The Complete Guide to

CIBACHROME®
PRINTING

The Complete Guide to

CIBACHROME® PRINTING

by Peter Krause and Henry A. Shull

ZIFF-DAVIS PUBLISHING COMPANY • NEW YORK

LIBRARY OF CONGRESS CATALOGUE CARD NUMBER: 80-51937
ISBN 0-87165-057-6 CLOTH; 0-87165-062-2 PAPER
PRINTED IN THE UNITED STATES OF AMERICA
FIRST PRINTING 1980
ZIFF-DAVIS PUBLISHING COMPANY
ONE PARK AVENUE
NEW YORK, N.Y. 10016

**TO JOAN
AND TO LORNA**

CONTENTS

Preface

A really expert craftsman not only has good tools and knows how to use them, he also has a thorough understanding of the basic system and of the materials with which he works. He knows their advantages and limitations and what affects their performance. In other words, he knows how to get the best out of all the parts that go into the final product.

All of his technical expertise, however, will not make him a great artist—that requires an inborn and nurtured talent in addition to good craftsmanship.

And so it is with color photography and color printing. A really fine color print is always the result of artistry combined with first-class workmanship. But how do you become an expert color printer? Well, there is no magical formula but it does require good tools, some knowledge of color technology, and a well-developed technique.

We believe that the Cibachrome® system is the best and the simplest color printing process available today and that anyone with reasonable manual dexterity can learn to make good Cibachrome prints. In fact, you could learn how to do this by reading the manufacturer's instruction leaflet and a trial-and-error method. If you want to make prints a cut above the average, however, you will have to know something more about why and how color printing works and how the Cibachrome process functions.

It is our aim to provide you with all of the really pertinent information on the technology and techniques involved in Cibachrome printing based on our own experience with the process and with color photography and printing in general. In fact, our ambition is even greater: We want to help you perceive the artistic potential of Cibachrome printing and stimulate your imagination so that you will make fine Cibachrome prints rather than just good ones. In any event, we are confident that once you get started in Cibachrome printing, you will discover a fascinating new world of personal expression whose boundaries will be set only by your own skill and imagination.

Cibachrome is a trademark of CIBA-GEIGY.

The Basic Elements of Color Printing

CHAPTER 1

Light and Color

If you are only a casual photographer, you are not likely to care about the technical intricacies of color photographic films or color printing. You just want to get pleasing color pictures as easily, inexpensively, and as quickly as possible; let others worry about the why and how. If you are sufficiently interested in color photography, however, to want to try your hand at color printing, you will sooner or later wonder why three color images are used in nearly all color photographic processes and why these images are usually yellow, magenta, and cyan in color. To understand the reasons for this tri-color scheme and the reasons for many other requirements in color printing, you must know something about the way our visual mechanism works. And that in turn involves light and how it interacts with our eyes and with objects around us.

It is for these reasons that a brief explanation is presented, first of some fundamental properties of light, color, and vision. These facts will help you in understanding and, therefore, in mastering the Cibachrome process.

The Nature of Light

Of the very wide gamut of electromagnetic radiation extending from high-frequency, short-wavelength cosmic rays to low-frequency, long radio waves, only a very small range is visible. This small range of radiation that can stimulate receptors in our eyes is called light.* Radiation that borders on the short wavelength end of light is called ultraviolet (UV), and that on the long wavelength end is called infrared (IR). These radiations, while not visible, are physically very similar to light and are of interest in photography because photographic materials have an inherent sensitivity to UV radiation and can be made to respond to IR radiation. (This is not to say that UV and IR radiations do not affect us in other ways—they do, as evidenced by a suntan or sunburn—but neither type can stimulate the receptors in our eyes; hence, neither can properly be called light.)

*Light radiation has a frequency of about 380 to 780×10^{12} cycles per second and a wavelength range of from 380 to 750 nanometers.

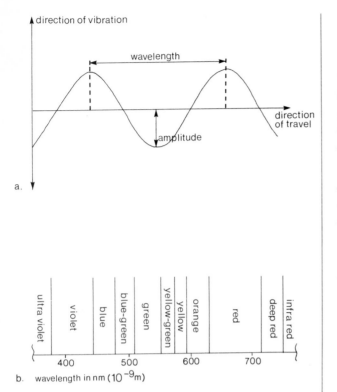

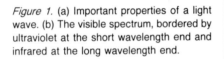

Figure 1. (a) Important properties of a light wave. (b) The visible spectrum, bordered by ultraviolet at the short wavelength end and infrared at the long wavelength end.

Like all other electromagnetic radiation, light interacts with different substances in various ways. Besides stimulating the light receptors in our eyes, it interacts with most substances and normally is partly reflected, partly absorbed, and often also partly transmitted by them. In this process it may be scattered and polarized (see Figure 2). The modulation of the incident light may also be selective with respect to wavelength, but all of these modifications of the radiation are due to the physical and chemical structure of the substances rather than physical differences in the light rays.

For example, sunlight falling onto freshly fallen snow is almost totally reflected and is scattered uniformly into all directions by the millions of differently shaped snow crystals at and below the surface. Therefore, the snow has the same neutral, white, bright appearance from every viewing angle. On the other hand, a shiny red boot seen against the snow looks that way because the material selectively absorbs a portion of the incident white light but diffusely reflects its red component. Red colorant particles incorporated in the material account for this selective absorption and the diffuse reflection. But the smooth surface also reflects nearly all of the incident light at and beyond a critical angle of incidence. The resultant specular reflections impart the appearance of glossiness to the material.

Absorbed light generally is converted to heat but it can, and often does, initiate other kinds of chemical and electrical actions, such as the bleaching of dyes or the changing of electrical conductivity in so-called photoconductors, as selenium used on a xerographic drum. It can even be re-radiated as longer wavelength light, as in certain types of fluorescence.

Materials that transmit a perceptible portion of light are called transparent or translucent, depending on the degree of scattering imparted to the transmitted beam. The physical and chemical properties of the material will determine the fraction of the total amount of incident light that is transmitted and the selectivity of transmission with respect to wavelength.

The Visual Mechanism and Color Perception

Human vision is very complex and incompletely understood. It involves stimulation of light receptors in our eyes; transmission of the consequent electrical signals to the brain by means of a massive network of nerves; and processing of the information at several stages, finally in the visual cortex of the brain (see Figure 3).

Notwithstanding this complexity and uncertainty, a simplified and useful model of vision can be constructed that explains adequately for the present purpose how we see and why we see different colors. This model also will help you to understand the basic function of color photographic materials and of color filters.

Our eyes are equipped with three optical elements—the cornea, aqueous humor, and variable-focus lens; together they form images of the objects in visual space to which the eyes are directed (see Figure 4). The image is focused onto the retina, a multi-layered membrane that contains two types of light-sensitive receptor cells—the rods and cones. These receptors are connected through a series of specialized cells with the fibers of the optical nerve bundle. The fovea centralis, a small spot near the center of the retina and on the optical axis, contains only tightly packed cone cells. It is the area of sharpest vision. The density of cones gradually diminishes from the fovea centralis outward, and the ratio of rods to cones gradually increases. The total number of light receptors, however, decreases substantially toward the periphery of the retina. This, coupled with optical aberrations and fewer nerve connections, makes for a decline in visual acuity toward the margins. But our eyes constantly scan objects of interest in the field of view and thereby yield a perceived image that is uniformly sharp throughout.

The rods have a broad range of response with peak sensitivity to light of about 500 nanometers, whereas the cones have three distinct narrower response functions (see Figure 5). The light sensitivity

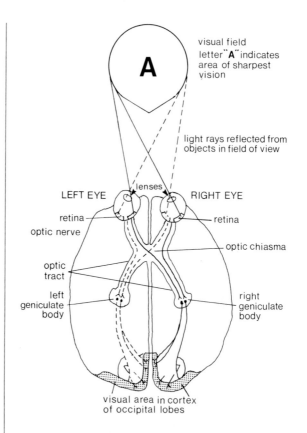

Figure 3. Simplified, schematic presentation of the main components involved in visual perception. Light rays entering each eye are focused on light receptors in the two retinas. The resultant nerve impulses travel to the optic chiasma where the two right halves and the two left halves of the image are combined. The signals are then relayed to the right and left occipital lobes. Visual perception results from the complex processing of these signals in the cortex of the brain. (From F. L. Ruch, *Psychology and Life*, Glenview, Ill., Scott, Foresman & Co., 1953, p. 415.)

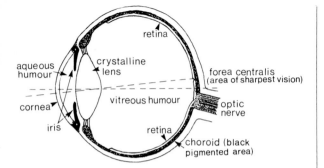

Figure 4. Schematic horizontal cross section of the human eye.

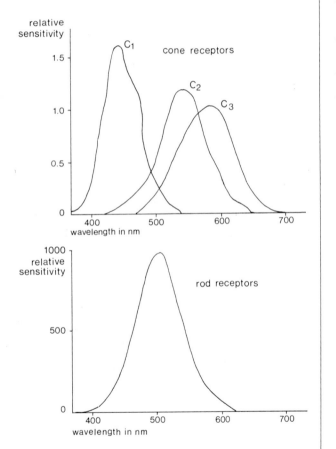

Figure 5. Approximate sensitivity curves of the rods and the three assumed types of cones in the human retina. Rods have about 1,000 times higher sensitivity than cones.

of the rods is about 1,000 times higher than that of the cones, but images generated by rod stimulation alone are rather unsharp and confined to shades of white, gray, and black—very much like a soft-focus, black-and-white photographic print image. Rod vision is called scotopic vision. At light intensity levels near 1/10 foot-candle, cone vision comes into play and with it our perception of chromatic colors and fine detail. Visual acuity and perceived color saturation increase with intensity of illumination up to a point. There is also a shift in color sensitivity that makes blue colors look brighter under low levels of illumination and red colors brighter under high levels. You can notice this effect when you point a spotlight onto a color print—red colors will suddenly appear much brighter and more saturated.

Pure cone vision is called photopic vision; it is the dominant mode under normal levels of outdoor and indoor illumination. As noted above, color vision is induced by the stimulation of the cones. More specifically, it is the relative intensity of stimulation of the three different types of cones that determines what color is seen. For example, a beam of light that contains wavelengths predominantly in the range of 400 to 500 nanometers will stimulate mostly cones having peak sensitivity in that portion of the spectrum, with the result that the light will look bluish to us. On the other hand, a light beam with a preponderance of 500-to-600 nm waves normally looks green, while one containing mostly waves beyond 600 nm in length looks red. In fact, it can be demonstrated readily that different wavelengths of light—or at least very narrow bands of wavelengths—elicit distinct color perceptions ranging from violet at the short-wavelength end to red at the long-wavelength end.

The colors of the light spectrum can be produced by passing a beam of white light through a glass prism that bends, or refracts, the short wavelengths more than the long ones and thereby spreads the white beam into a multihued band (see Figure 6). This classic demonstration, first made by Sir Isaac Newton, led Thomas Young later on to postulate that we have a trichromatic type of visual response mechanism. In time, precise measurements of the response of individual receptors to light of different wavelengths yielded the rod and cone sensitivity curves reproduced in Figure 5. The assumption, however, that the perception of blue, green, and red is simply and directly related to the intensity of stimulation of the three types of cones has proven to be incorrect. The visual process is much more complex than that and the perception of color involves and depends upon interactions among all the signals from all receptors. Nevertheless, the primary stimulation is of a tri-chromatic kind, and it is common and appropriate, therefore, to call blue, green, and red the primary colors.

Light Sources and Object Colors

Vision and photography require the presence of light under normal circumstances. Outdoors you normally see and take pictures by the light emitted by the sun. Indoors tungsten filament lamps are often used and occasionally flash lamps. All of these light sources are of the incandescent type: that means they radiate light because their temperature is above a certain critical level. For example, if an iron poker is placed into a coal fire, it will start to emit invisible infrared radiation at a certain temperature. Increasingly shorter waves will be emitted as the temperature continues to rise and at a temperature of about 700°C the iron will begin to show a dull red glow. With further increases in temperature the poker will turn bright red (red hot), then yellow, and finally a bluish-white color (white hot). The total amount of radiation also will increase with temperature, and as a consequence the iron will look much brighter when bluish-white than when dull red. Moreover, at any one temperature the radiation will encompass a continuous range of wavelengths from infrared through the visible.

Because of this definite relation between the temperature of a material and the energy distribution of its emitted light that is independent of the material structure, the color of an incandescent source can be associated with its temperature. The red-glowing iron poker has a low color temperature whereas sunlight has a relatively high color temperature. Color temperature values usually are given in degrees Kelvin, or K. The Kelvin temperature, based on absolute zero, can be converted to centigrade by adding 273.

The color temperature values of several light sources important in everyday life and in photography are given in the table below:

LIGHT SOURCE	APPROX. COLOR TEMPERATURE
100W tungsten lamp	2,870K (3,143°C)
85W quartz iodine lamp	3,075K (3,148°C)
Clear photoflash lamp	3,500K (3,773°C)
Sunlight at noon (winter) 40°N	5,075K (5,348°C)
Sunlight at noon (summer) 40°N	5,750K (6,023°C)
Electronic flash lamp	6,000K (6,273°C)

Besides incandescent light sources, there are others that are of increasing importance in home and outdoor lighting and in photography. Most of these are based on the effects of an electric discharge in a gas (neon, argon, xenon) enclosed in a glass envelope. The emission of light by these types of sources results from the violent collision of atoms and ions of the gas brought about by the passage of the electric current. The radiation from such gaseous light sources is confined to a few wavelengths of light (line spectrum) rather than being continuous as from incandescent sources (continuous spectrum).

Fluorescent lamps are a special kind of gas-discharge lamp in which the inner wall of the glass envelope is coated with a mixture of light-emitting phosphor particles. Mercury gas inside the tube is excited by an electrical discharge and radiates discrete lines of violet, green, and red light, but also a sizable amount of ultraviolet radiation. This UV radiation is strongly absorbed by the phosphor particles and stimulates them to emit a continuous range of colors. As a result, the total light emitted by fluorescent lamps is a mixture of a gaseous line spectrum and a continuous-fluorescence light spectrum. (You are unaware of this peculiarity when you look at a fluorescent lamp, but some objects take on unexpected colors under fluorescent lighting, and color photographs often show poor color renditions for this reason, unless color correction filters are used.)

Spectral energy distribution curves for a typical fluorescent lamp, a tungsten lamp, and sunlight are shown in Figure 7. Note the peculiar combination of continuous and line emissions in the fluorescent lamp spectrum compared with the uniform distribution of energy throughout the visible region in the other two spectra.

Light emitted by a light source will radiate outward in all directions unless its propagation is modified by a reflector, an enclosure, or some other optical element (lens, prism). As noted, it will interact with objects in its path and be partially or totally reflected, absorbed, or transmitted by them. Most objects modulate light in a quite constant manner and therefore have a unique and characteristic appearance. This encourages us to think of objects as having definite colors, just as they tend to have definite sizes and shapes. For example, you expect grass to be green, clear sky to be blue, and concrete to be gray. This prompts us to speak and think of object colors—something that belongs to them. Of course, green grass could not and would not look green under red light, but it will maintain its normal, expected color under a surprising variety of lighting conditions. For instance, we are not conscious most of the time of any change in the color of an object as we move from daylight into tungsten illumination, even though daylight contains relatively much more blue light than tungsten light. This remarkable quality of our visual system is termed color constancy and sometimes adaptation, but adaptation also covers our unconscious adjustment to changes in the intensity of illumination.

Color photographic materials do not have this faculty of adaptation, and light of a very definite color distribution must be used in exposing any given product; otherwise the overall color balance of the photographic image will be incorrect and objects will be reproduced off-color. Some of these factors were involved in a rather humorous and interesting incident that occurred during the *Explorer II* satellite mission to Mars. When the first multi-spectral television signals transmitted back from the Martian surface were converted into color prints, the sky had a pink color. This was thought to be due to a technical flaw since, obviously, sky should be blue in color. Consequently, the prints were remade with an appropriate correction in color balance. Only later was it realized that the Martian atmosphere would indeed make its sky look pink and that the first set of prints showed the correct colors.

Having considered how we see color and why we associate certain colors with certain objects, we should examine in somewhat greater detail why objects look as they do. For instance, why do a green filter and a green leaf look green? A simplified schematic presentation is shown in Figure 8. Here, white light, which is shown to be a mixture of the primary blue-, green-, and red-light components, falls onto the filter in one instance and the leaf in the other. The filter transmits and the leaf reflects only the green portion, and both absorb the blue and red portions; therefore, both look green. A more accurate explanation is given in Figure 9, showing the wavelength distribution of the light that has passed through the filter and that which has been reflected by the leaf. A moment's consideration will make you appreciate that it is these portions of the light that will reach our eyes and will account for what we actually see. You will note that both curves have a peak near 510 to 520 nanometers, accounting for the green color of these two materials. Similarly, a red object will absorb primarily blue and green light and reflect red, while a blue object will selectively absorb green and red light and reflect a significantly higher proportion of blue light (see Figure 10).

Additive and Subtractive Color Mixtures

We have seen that white light is a mixture of the three primary colors—blue, green, and red. Now examine what happens when the primary colors are mixed in different proportions. It would seem logical to start with mixtures of equal parts of two primaries. The results of such mixing are illustrated in Figure 11. The colors yellow, magenta, and cyan that are obtained in this fashion are well known to color photographers because they are the colors of the dyes used in most color camera films and in all color print materials to generate the final color images. As shown in Figure 12, yellow, magenta, and cyan are also called complementary

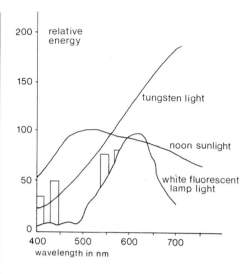

Figure 7. Spectral distribution curves showing the relative amounts of energy in three different types of white light. The values have been adjusted to permit plotting of all three curves in one graph. Normally, sunlight would have by far the greatest amount of total energy. Note the line spectrum superposed on the continuous spectrum of the fluorescent light source.

colors because each complements a primary color to form white light. Another name for the complementary colors is subtractive primaries because each subtracts one primary color from a white light mixture.

As a next step, consider the mixtures of two parts of one primary light with one part of another and then that of other proportions of two and all three primaries. Some of the results of such light-mixing experiments are tabulated in the table below:

CONSTITUENTS OF LIGHT MIXTURE	COLOR OF MIXTURE
2 parts blue + 1 part red	purple
2 parts green + 1 part red	chartreuse
1/2 part blue + 1 part green + 1 part red	brown
1/2 part blue + 1/2 part green + 1 part red	brick red
1/2 part blue + 1/2 part green + 1/2 part red	gray

Actually, nearly all object colors contain a mixture of all wavelengths of the visible spectrum, but their distribution varies, as illustrated in Figures 9 and 10. The predominant wavelengths in such a mixture determine the hue of the color (blue, green, yellow), the ratio of the dominant to the other wavelengths determines the saturation of the color (deep or pale green), while the intensity of the light determines the lightness of the color (dark or light green).

But what happens when subtractive primaries are mixed? This question is of importance when printing filters are used in color printing.

Color Filters

Color filters are transparent pieces of glass or plastic material that have been treated so as to selectively transmit some wavelengths of light more than others. To do this, they must obviously reflect or absorb the unwanted wavelengths. Interference- or dichroic-type filters reflect the unwanted wavelengths, whereas stained glass or dyed plastic filters absorb them. A portion of all the incident light is always reflected from the filter surface, the amount depending on the angle of incidence and the refractive index of the material. (A small amount of light will also be back-scattered from within the mass of the filter, but generally this component can be neglected.) A graph that shows the relationship between transmitted, absorbed, and reflected light for a dyed-green gelatin filter is reproduced in Figure 13.

In color printing, three different kinds of filters are normally used—color compensating filters, infrared absorbing filters, and ultraviolet absorbing filters. The color compensating filters are needed in a range of yellow, magenta, and cyan densities in order to provide the required control over the amounts of blue, green, and red light in the printing light. The infrared filter keeps heat rays from the color film and the filters, thereby minimizing film buckling and fading of the dyes in the color filters. The ultraviolet absorbing filter cuts out short wavelength radiation transmitted by many color image dyes that would tend to interfere with proper color reproduction in the print image.

Yellow, magenta, and cyan printing filters are available in sets from several manufacturers and come in different sizes and optical quality. Each color series normally contains six filters numbered 05, 10, 20, 30, 40, and 50, providing a stepped ascension in light absorption. As shown in Figure 14, each step of ten effects a reduction of blue-, green-, or red-light transmittance of about 20 percent. The number 30 filter of each series, in consequence, reduces the intensity of its complementary color by about 50 percent.

Inasmuch as each of the subtractive-type color filters controls one primary color, two types together will control two primary colors. For example, if a number 30 yellow filter is combined with a number 30 magenta filter, the combination will reduce the intensity of the blue and green light components by 50 percent, and only the red light component will remain essentially unaffected. The results obtained by combining various subtractive filters are delineated in Figure 15. You should note that a combination of yellow, magenta, and cyan filters yields neutral density, which merely reduces light intensity without significant change in color quality—it should be avoided, therefore, under normal circumstances.

Modern color enlargers often are equipped with special color heads. These may contain one or more lamp(s) and a set of yellow, magenta, and cyan interference filters, also called dichroic filters; or they may have three lamps—one filtered by a blue, one by a green, and one by a red filter. The light from these lamps usually is mixed in a light box and then directed downward onto the film image. Color heads offer two main advantages over enlargers in which individual, dyed color filters are used in a filter tray. Firstly, the interference-type filters will not fade with use as all dyed filters do; and, secondly, an interference filter system provides infinite adjustments in color balance within the wide limits imposed by the response characteristics of the printing material and the optical components. Of course, dyed filters are less expensive and can be used with almost any enlarger.

The questions as to why and how color filters are used in Cibachrome printing will be answered in some detail in Chapter 7.

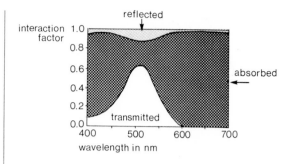

Figure 13. Curves showing the reflection, absorption, and transmission characteristics of a green filter. (After R. M. Evans, *An Introduction to Color*, New York, John Wiley & Sons, Inc., 1948, p. 59.)

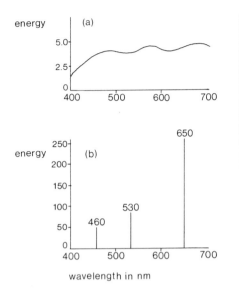

Figure 16. Spectral composition of two halves of the field of view in a color measuring instrument when the light of (a) is matched by a mixture of monochromatic lines at 460, 530, and 650 nm wavelength (b). (From W. D. Wright, *The Measurement of Colour*, New York, Van Nostrand Reinhold Co., 1969, p. 139.)

Control of Colors and Permissible Tolerances

Among the many remarkable qualities of our visual system is its capability of detecting color differences as small as one percent in a side-by-side comparison. It is for this reason that visual color grading and color matching are still the preferred methods of sorting in several sectors of agriculture and industry. Our eyes are not analytical instruments, however, and we cannot tell by looking at a scene what the wavelength compositions of its colors are. An extreme example of this inability to distinguish wavelength composition is illustrated in Figure 16: the light composed of the continuous distribution of wavelength looks the same as that made up of three discrete wavelengths. It is fortunate that our vision functions in this manner and not like our hearing which allows us to identify different musical instruments playing the same note, owing to our ability to discern the different overtones in the mixed sound waves. We could not have the color photographic processes of today or any other of the simple color reproduction systems, such as color TV, if it were not for the fact that satisfactory color matches can be obtained with a rather wide range of light distributions, rather than requiring a wavelength-by-wavelength match.

Two colors that match visually but have different spectral distribution are called a metameric pair. To the extent that the spectral differences are not very great, such pairs will also tend to match under different types of illumination. The greater these differences, however, the greater the probability that the match made under one illumination will not hold under another and the greater the likelihood that someone else will not agree with your judgment. This is an important aspect of color vision because the dyes used in some color print materials, including those in Cibachrome-A print material, tend to shift noticeably in hue when viewed under different types of illumination. You may have to consider this factor when matching prints and transparencies or when making color prints for exhibition. To avoid any unpleasant surprises, it is always best to judge color photographic images by the light that is to be used ultimately for viewing.

Small color differences are readily noticed in a side-by-side comparison, but it is difficult to make a match without a reference sample. For example, you can easily see small differences in shades of white among a dozen eggs, but you would have great problems in a paint shop selecting a matching color to touch up your walls at home without a reference swatch. This is so because our absolute judgment of colors is imprecise and our color memory only approximate. Nevertheless, we do have memory colors and these influence our judgment concerning the correctness of color reproduction. For instance, everyone seems to have fairly definite ideas about the *true* color of blue sky, of skin, of green grass, and of other familiar objects; we expect and want the colors of photographic reproductions to approximate these memory colors. Interestingly enough, the preferred flesh-tone reproduction is more yellowish than actual skin color, and the favored reproduction of blue sky is brighter and more saturated than most normal daytime skies really are.

These and other characteristics of the visual system make it virtually impossible and rather unrewarding to attempt specifying the requirements of *accurate* color reproduction in color photographic images. It is not a problem to the practical photographer, however, and it imposes no real limitation on your opportunity of making excellent Cibachrome prints. After all, you will want to make prints that are aesthetically pleasing or even provocative rather than exact matches of the original scene, whatever that may mean.

CHAPTER 2

Color Photography

Basic Process—Color Analysis and Synthesis

During the more than one hundred years that color photographic processes and materials have been proposed and produced, a large variety of color reproduction methods have been described and many tried. Significant use and success, however, have been enjoyed only by a few additive-type camera color-plates and films in the period from 1907 to 1940 and by a rather small number of subtractive-type color film and reflection print processes since 1935. These commercially viable color processes have been, and are, trichromatic processes, that is, systems in which all image colors are produced by means of only three colors. It is not surprising, of course, that a trichromatic reproduction process should offer the best combination of color reproduction quality and simplicity, since our visual response mechanism is trichromatic with response peaks in the blue, green, and red portions of the light spectrum.

The reproduction of colors by a trichromatic photographic process involves two basic steps—color analysis and color synthesis. Color analysis encompasses the formation of three component images, one of which is a record of the blue content of the original, one of its green content, and one of its red content. The making of these three color separation images simulates the first step of our visual process in which the three types of cones in the retina respond differentially to the blue, green, and red light intensities in the image focused onto the retina by the optical elements of the eye. In a subtractive-type photographic color process, three separate light-sensitive layers take the place of the three types of cones, one layer responding primarily to the blue portion of the visible spectrum, one to the green portion, and one to the red portion.

In modern color materials, these three layers are very thin and are coated one on top of the other in optical contact and in an inseparable assembly. The topmost layer of such a material normally is sensitive primarily to blue light, the middle layer chiefly to green light, and the bottom layer to red light. A yellow filter layer is positioned below the top layer to prevent blue light from reaching the two lower layers that have inherent blue sensitivity in addition to their imparted green or red sensitivity, as shown in Figure 17. (Another layer arrangement with the red-sensitive layer on top and the blue-sensitive layer on the bottom is used in color papers made for the printing of masked color negatives. The required isolation of the blue, green, and red response functions is achieved in such papers by a wide separation in sensitivity levels between the blue-sensitive bottom layer and the other two layers.)

When a multilayer photographic material of this type is exposed to a color image in a camera or printer and then developed in a black-and-white developer, three superposed negative silver images are formed that are of equal size and in perfect register. They are records of the blue, green, and red light-intensity patterns of the original color image and are called the blue, green, and red color-separation images.

In the second basic reproduction step called color synthesis, the three negative images are utilized to produce three positive color images that in combination provide that mixture of blue, green, and/or red light at each image point that is required for the reproduction, or synthesis, of the original color.

Subtractive and Additive Processes

When the three separation images are superposed, as they are in nearly all modern color photographic materials, the blue-separation positive must be transformed into a yellow image because a yellow colorant absorbs blue, but not green or red light. Hence, the positive yellow image modulates the blue light intensity without affecting the green and red light intensities. Similarly, the green separation positive must be converted into a magenta image, which will modulate only green light; and the red separation positive must be converted into a cyan image, which modulates red light.

The manufacture of multilayer color materials is a very complex task that has required many discoveries in dye and processing chemistry as well as major developments in photographic emulsion-making and coating. For these reasons, simpler if less satisfactory additive materials were made and

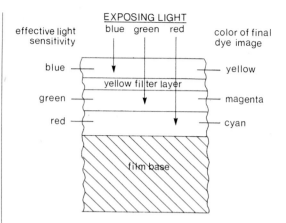

Figure 17. Basic layer arrangement of a subtractive-type color photographic material. The light-sensitive image layers typically are from two to four microns thick and contain silver halide crystals and color formers or dyes dispersed in a gelatin matrix. The yellow filter layer prevents blue light from reaching the two bottom layers, which have inherent sensitivity to blue light. The filter layer is decolorized during processing.

used in the early days of color photography. The most successful of these utilized a single light-sensitive layer coated on top of a mosaic filter layer that contained adjacent blue, green, and red filter elements. Exposure of such a plate or film produced juxtaposed color separation negative images. The negative silver images were removed, and complementary positive silver images formed by means of re-exposure and a second development step. These positive silver images modulated the intensity of the white viewing light before it reached the filter mosaic layer. The final image colors were perceived as a result of integration by the eye of the juxtaposed blue, green, and/or red dots of varying intensity, the individual filter elements being below the resolution threshold under normal viewing conditions.

A simplified presentation of color analysis and color synthesis in an additive and a subtractive color reproduction scheme is given in Figure 18.

Color Transparencies and Color Reflection Prints

Color photographic materials are available on transparent and on white opaque supports and for some special display applications also on white translucent supports.

Color transparencies may be wanted for direct viewing on an illuminator or for projection onto a screen or as printing masters. A color negative film image is a typical printing master that serves as an intermediate in the production of the desired final color photograph, be it a reflection color print, such as a Kodacolor print, or a positive color transparency. Positive color transparencies, however, such as 35mm slides, may also serve as printing masters, as in Cibachrome printing.

Reflection color prints usually are made from color transparency images by projection or contact printing, but may be direct copies of other photographic color prints or reproductions of original art work or even of three-dimensional objects. Reflection print images require less than half the color densities of transparency images, because light must pass through the print image layers twice and is reflected incompletely and diffusely from the white opaque support.

Images on white translucent supports may be viewed by transmitted or reflected light but have less than optimum quality under either viewing condition.

Negative-Positive and Direct-Positive Color Reproduction Processes

Color photographs, like black-and-white photographs, can be produced by negative-positive or direct-positive methods. In a typical color negative-positive system, a color negative film is exposed in the camera and then processed to form a negative color image. In a subsequent printing step, a color paper or color print film is exposed through the color negative film image, then processed like the color negative, and yields a final positive image. In a direct-positive color system, the exposed material is developed first in a black-and-white developer to form three black-and-white separation images and then treated to produce three positive dye images in the same material.

The color negative-positive process has become the dominant photographic color reproduction system since the introduction of integral color masking in Kodak Kodacolor and Ektacolor films. This feature makes it possible to automatically obtain good color reproduction in color prints made from color negatives. In combination with the great exposure latitude that can be built into camera negative films, it represents a very satisfactory system for the mass amateur market as well as for professional applications where many prints are wanted from one negative.

However, direct-positive color materials, such as Kodachrome, Agfachrome, Fujichrome, and Ektachrome films, have always maintained an important place in color photography because they provide the best image quality attainable with a color photographic film. Consequently, such films have been preferred for 35mm slides and other applications where only one high-quality record is desired, such as home movies, or where high-quality reproductions are to be made from the photographic image by some graphic arts process, such as magazine and book publishing. More recently, the advent of the Cibachrome print system has provided significant additional usefulness and appeal in regard to direct-positive color transparencies.

Formation of the Color Image

The formation of the yellow, magenta, and cyan dye images is achieved in most modern color photographic materials by color coupling development. This involves so-called color couplers that combine with an oxidized color developing agent to form dyes. The color couplers may be incorporated into the light-sensitive layers of the photographic material during manufacture (incorporated coupler types such as Agfacolor and Ektachrome) or introduced during processing (Kodachrome). The color developing agent must be capable of reducing exposed silver halides to metallic silver, and its oxidized reaction product must be capable of combining or coupling with the color couplers to produce the required yellow, magenta, and cyan dyes. Materials that utilize this kind of color formation are also known as *chromogenic*-type materials.

The Cibachrome dye-bleach system is fundamentally different from chromogenic systems in that the image dyes are incorporated in the material in their final, colorful state during manufacture. They are destroyed image-wise during processing through the action of a bleach catalyst that is rendered active by the silver of the negative image produced during an initial processing step. The amount of dye that is bleached is proportional to the amount of negative image silver; hence, the process yields a positive dye image directly.

Reversal-Type Color Films

In view of the importance in Cibachrome printing of Kodachrome- and Ektachrome-type slides, it seems appropriate to review their process of image formation in somewhat greater detail.

As shown schematically in Figure 19, Kodachrome film is a multilayer material having blue-, green-, and red-sensitive layers coated in superposition on a transparent film base.

The usual yellow filter layer between the blue- and green-sensitive emulsions prevents blue light from reaching the lower layers. After exposure, the film is developed in a black-and-white developer to yield the blue-, green-, and red-separation negative images. It is then exposed uniformly from the back to red light and developed in a developing solution that contains a color-developing agent as well as a cyan dye coupler. The developing agent reduces the exposed silver halides in the bottom layer to metallic silver. The developer byproducts formed by the silver-reducing action combine, or couple, with the cyan color coupler that has diffused into the layer to form a positive cyan dye image in the immediate vicinity of the positive silver image. In the next step the film is re-exposed uniformly by blue light from the front and then treated in a developer that contains a yellow dye coupler. A positive silver and a positive yellow dye image are formed. Then a positive silver and magenta dye image are produced in a third color-developing step with a solution containing a developing agent and a magenta dye coupler. Finally, all the silver and residual chemicals are removed by bleaching, fixing, and washing, with the result that only the three super-posed yellow, magenta, and cyan dye images remain.

Even though Kodachrome processing has been simplified and improved, it is still very complex and requires elaborate chemical and photographic controls. A much simpler method—pioneered by Agfa—was subsequently adopted for all other chromogenic color materials. It utilizes incorporated, non-diffusing color couplers, that is, colorless dye form-ers that are dispersed in the appropriate light-sensitive layers during manufacture. These couplers can be transformed into yellow, magenta and cyan dyes in a single color-developing step through reaction with the oxidation byproducts of one color-developing agent. The basic construction of such a material and the main steps of positive color image formation are delineated in Figure 19.

Several different techniques have been developed for preventing incorporated color couplers as well as the final dye molecules from wandering from one layer to another. In the Agfa system the size of the coupler and dye molecules is enlarged by linked chemical groups which render them substantive to the emulsion gelatin and non-diffusing. In the Kodak Ektachrome and similar systems, ballasted dye molecules are first dissolved in a hydrophobic solvent and then dispersed in the emulsion gelatin in the form of microscopic droplets. The Ektachrome system offers a number of advantages which have made it the preferred system for most chromogenic color materials of the incorporated coupler type.

Differences Between Color Materials

Although nearly all modern color photographic materials are based on the same basic principles of color analysis and color synthesis, and although the yellow, magenta, and cyan dyes used for image formation are similar in structure and perform the same function, there are differences in the chemical and physical properties of different dye images that affect their visual as well as their printing qualities. Moreover, the keeping quality and stability of the dye images in dark and light storage and under different ambient conditions can and do differ appreciably.

Of particular interest in color printing are the spectral absorption properties of these dyes and the differences between various dye sets. Ideally, the yellow, magenta, and cyan image dyes should absorb light only in their assigned regions of the visible spectrum. However, actual dyes that are useful and usable in color photography absorb appreciable amounts of light that they should transmit completely. Cyan dyes tend to be particularly deficient in that they absorb green and blue light to a significant extent. Magenta dyes also absorb blue light excessively. Only yellow dyes come close to the desired color quality standards. The light absorption curves of an ideal and of a typical actual set of yellow, magenta, and cyan image dyes are shown in Figure 20.

The net result of the unwanted spectral absorptions of the image dyes is a loss of color quality in the photographic reproduction. This kind of image degradation is of particular concern in color printing because the deficiencies of the dyes in the print master are compounded by those used in the printing materials. Fortunately, the problem has been overcome to a major extent in modern materials through application of color-masking techniques. In color negative films this has taken the form of colored couplers that produce low-contrast positive images in the cyan and magenta dye layers that effectively cancel the unwanted secondary absorptions of the main dye images. In direct-positive color materials, controlled chemical interactions between image layers are utilized to achieve the desired effects during processing. A process of this kind is used in Cibachrome print materials and especially in the newest self-masking type of products. An explanation of this masking method is given in the next chapter.

CHAPTER 3

The Cibachrome Process

Principal Features of the Process

The Cibachrome process is a direct-positive process based on the dye-bleach principle. In this process yellow, magenta, and cyan azo dyes incorporated in the color photographic material during manufacture are bleached during processing. The extent of bleaching is proportional to the mass of negative image silver obtained through light exposure and subsequent chemical development. The silver compounds and other chemical byproducts of processing are removed in a fixing and washing step following dye bleaching, leaving a direct-positive azo-dye image.

The basic structure of a Cibachrome printing material and the main functions of its components are depicted in the schematic drawing in Figure 21; the principal steps of the Cibachrome process are outlined in Figure 22. The key step in the process is the dye-bleaching step. It involves complex chemical reactions in which a mobile bleach catalyst is first reduced on interacting with metallic silver grains of the negative image. The reduced catalyst, in turn, bleaches the azo dye surrounding the grains and in doing so is re-oxidized and reactivated. The catalyst can be visualized as shuttling back and forth between silver grains and dye molecules, both of which are imbedded in the gelatin layer and are immobile. The net result of these reactions is the formation of a *bleach halo* around each silver grain, as shown schematically in Figure 23. The catalyst is active only over a given distance from the grain, thus limiting the size of the bleach halo that constitutes the basic image element of the final dye image.

The number of bleach halos formed in each dye layer is directly related to the number of silver grains, but the amount of reduced, or bleached, dye is super-proportional—that is, a relatively small mass of silver effects a considerable reduction of dye. This provides an efficient system and one where a low-contrast negative silver image yields a positive dye image of much higher contrast and density range (see Figure 24). Of course, the characteristics of the negative silver image of a specific Cibachrome material must be chosen so as to produce a positive dye image that has good whites and blacks and good tone reproduction. If the negative image is too low in density range or contrast, veiled highlights or insufficient contrast will be obtained in the dye image. High negative contrast or high silver fog, on the other hand, will yield excessively high contrast or low maximum density in the final dye image.

Differences Between the Cibachrome Process and Other Color Processes and Materials

It will be evident from the foregoing that the Cibachrome process functions in opposite fashion from conventional chromogenic processes. In the Cibachrome process image dyes are destroyed, whereas in chromogenic processes they are produced in proportion to developed silver. This makes the dye-bleach system simpler and more elegant for direct-positive reproduction when negative-working silver halide emulsions are employed for the formation of three separation negative images. Chromogenic materials that incorporate such emulsions require a more complex reversal processing procedure to yield positive images.

Another difference stems from the types of dyes that are utilized in the dye-bleach and in chromogenic systems. The azo dyes employed in Cibachrome materials are inherently more stable than the azo-methine and indo-aniline type dyes used in chromogenic systems. Furthermore, most chromogenic-type photographs contain residual color couplers that can discolor with time, whereas properly processed Cibachrome prints are free of any potential degradation substances. Consequently, Cibachrome images have exceptionally good dark and light stability and are more resistant to staining and fading by industrial gases and other atmospheric pollutants than chromogenic-type dyes.

Refer to Chapter 11 for a detailed discussion of the keeping quality of Cibachrome images and of recommended display and storage conditions.

Other Advantages of the Cibachrome Process

Cibachrome dyes also have very good spectrophotometric characteristics and therefore yield images having excellent color saturation and hue rendition. Moreover, the presence of the color dyes in the emulsion layers minimizes light scattering within the layers during exposure. This ensures high resolution and good image sharpness. Other advantages are as follows:

- The color print material has soft gradation and a long exposure scale that afford great latitude in print exposure and filtration.
- The latent image is very stable; processing can be delayed for days without noticeable change in image quality.
- The chemical process is short and simple and tailored to home darkroom as well as professional application.
- Tolerance limits for processing times and solution temperatures are wide.
- The processing solutions have good shelf life in their original, sealed containers; they also maintain their activity in ready-to-use concentration for weeks when properly stored.

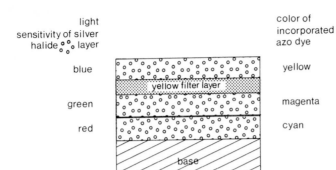

light
sensitivity of silver
halide layer

blue

green

red

color of
incorporated
azo dye

yellow

yellow filter layer

magenta

cyan

base

Figure 21. Basic structure of Cibachrome print materials. Additional layers are used in present products to modify various photographic characteristics.

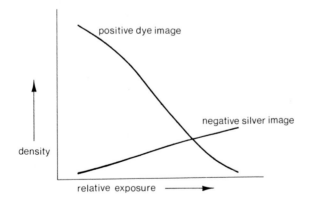

positive dye image

negative silver image

density

relative exposure

Figure 24. In the Cibachrome process a low-contrast negative silver image is formed first. The azo dyes incorporated in the material during manufacture are then bleached in proportion to the amount of silver, yielding a positive dye image which has higher contrast and a greater density range than the negative silver image. The final print image has the desired contrast for good tone and color reproduction.

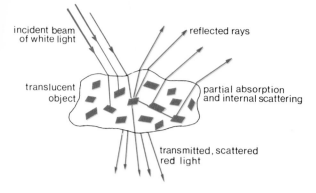

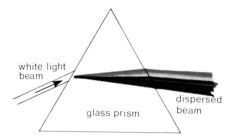

Figure 2. Schematic illustration of the interaction of light with a translucent object. The incident white light is partially reflected, partially absorbed, and partially transmitted. The rough surface reflects part of all the wavelengths of the incident white light. Red light is also back-scattered from below the surface; together with the white light it makes the object look reddish. The transmitted red light is less diluted with white light when the object is held up against the light; therefore, the color seen by transmitted light is a deeper red. Because the light is scattered considerably on passing through the object, the material is translucent rather than transparent.

Figure 6. A collimated beam of white light is refracted by the glass prism and dispersed into its component colors. Short wavelengths are refracted more than long wavelengths, producing the familiar rainbow arrangement of the visible spectrum.

Figure 8. Simplified, schematic presentation of the interaction of a white light beam with a green filter (a) and with a green leaf (b).

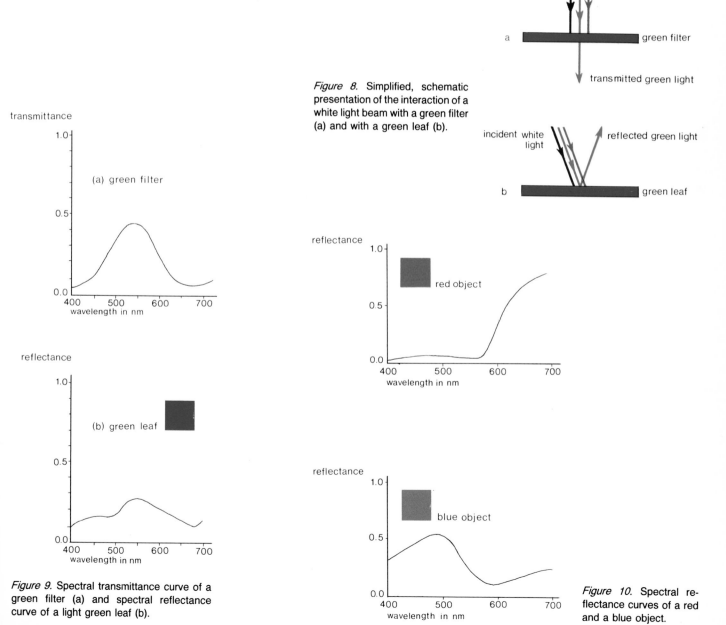

Figure 9. Spectral transmittance curve of a green filter (a) and spectral reflectance curve of a light green leaf (b).

Figure 10. Spectral reflectance curves of a red and a blue object.

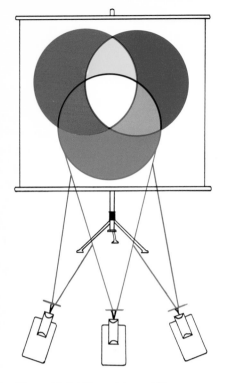

Figure 11. Additive mixture of blue, green and red light yields:
yellow . . . in the mixture of green and red
magenta . . . in the mixture of blue and red
cyan . . . in the mixture of blue and green
white . . . in the mixture of blue, green, and red.

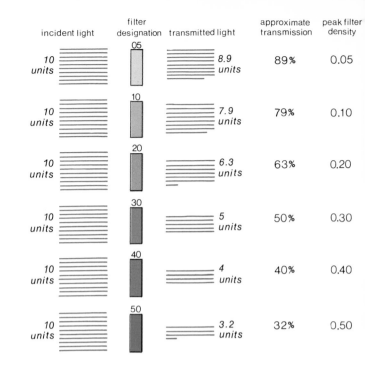

incident light	filter designation	transmitted light	approximate transmission	peak filter density
10 units	05	8.9 units	89%	0.05
10 units	10	7.9 units	79%	0.10
10 units	20	6.3 units	63%	0.20
10 units	30	5 units	50%	0.30
10 units	40	4 units	40%	0.40
10 units	50	3.2 units	32%	0.50

Figure 14. Schematic illustration of the relations between the filter numbers, the approximate green light transmittances, and the peak densities of a typical series of magenta printing filters. The corresponding yellow and cyan filter series have equivalent values for blue or red light. Note that the filter designation is derived from its peak density value.

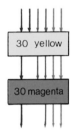

Figure 15. Control over the color of light obtained through use of combinations of number 30 color-printing filters. The three-filter combination is not employed as a rule because it merely reduces light intensity without significant change in color quality.

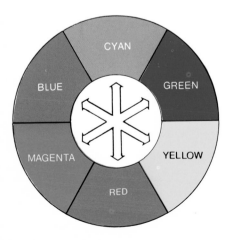

Figure 12. The three primary and the three complementary colors obtained by mixing blue, green, and red light.

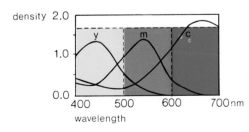

Figure 20. Light modulation by a set of theoretical (dashed lines) and a set of real (solid lines) yellow (y), magenta (m), and cyan (c) dyes used in color photography.

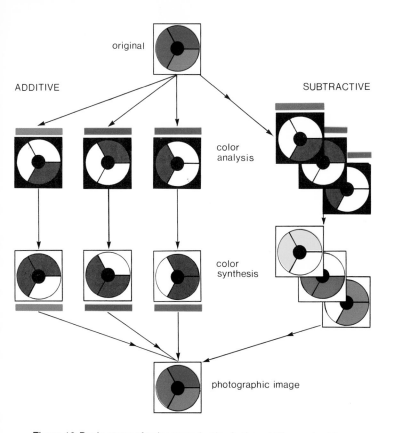

Figure 18. Basic steps of color reproduction in the additive and subtractive systems.

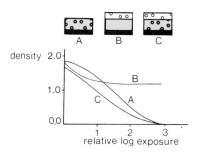

1. exposure to a positive color image
2. b&w development
3. dye & silver bleaching
4. fixing
5. washing and drying

Figure 22. The main steps in Cibachrome print-making.

density 2.0

relative log exposure

Figure 26. Control over speed and gradation can be obtained in Cibachrome materials through the use of adjacent undyed silver halide emulsion layers. In this example, layer A, which contains silver halides and a yellow azo dye, yields sensitometric curve A with normal processing. When the silver halides are incorporated in a separate, adjacent layer, as in B, remote bleaching of the dye produces sensitometric curve B. The combination of A and B, as in arrangement C, produces the sensitometric curve C. The gradation of C is better than that of curve A, and C also has higher speed (displacement to the left).

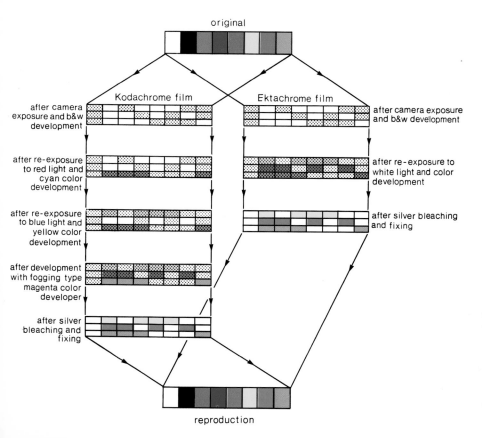

Figure 19. Main processing steps for two types of reversal color films. After camera exposure both types are developed in a black-and-white developer to produce negative separation images in the blue, green, and red sensitive layers. Thereafter, Ektachrome-type films require only a single re-exposure (or chemical fogging) and one-color development because the yellow, magenta, and cyan dye formers are incorporated in the layers during manufacture.
Kodachrome film requires selective re-exposure and color development. The final processing steps for both film types are silver bleaching, fixing, washing, and drying.

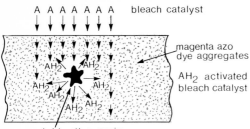

Figure 23. Schematic presentation of the basic dye-bleach reaction used in the Cibachrome process. A bleach catalyst contained in a suitably compounded bleach solution diffuses into the image layer and reacts with the metallic silver particles previously formed in the layer by exposure and development. After reaction with the silver grain, the bleach catalyst diffuses outward and bleaches the surrounding azo dye. A bleach halo is formed around the grain. This halo is the primary image element in the final Cibachrome print, from which the silver particles have been removed by silver bleaching, fixing and washing.

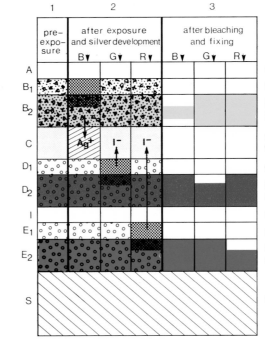

Figure 25. Cross section of Cibachrome-A print material. The undyed blue, green and red sensitive layers are employed to secure improved speed and tone reproduction in the associated dyed image layers. The yellow filter layer prevents blue light from reaching the green and red sensitive layers, which have inherent sensitivity to blue light.

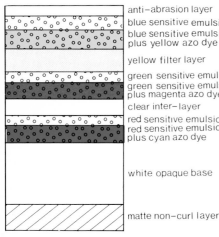

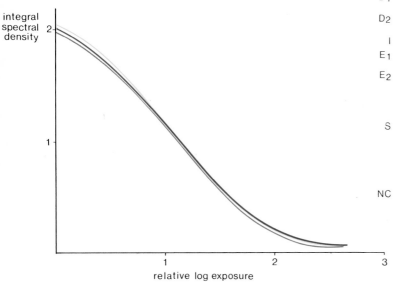

Figure 28. Cross section of the new self-masked Cibachrome print material. A positive silver mask image is formed in layer C, whose density is controlled by reaction products formed during development in the sensitized layers B_1B_2, D_1D_2 and E_1E_2. (See text for a detailed explanation.)

Figure 27. Sensitometric curves of a Cibachrome print derived from a neutral gray scale image.

Figure 29. The self-masking process of the new Cibachrome II—Process P-3 system.

1. Before exposure:
The two blue-sensitive emulsions B_1 and B_2 contain silver bromide grains. The green- and red-sensitive emulsions D_1, D_2, E_1, and E_2 contain silver bromo-iodide grains. The yellow filter (and masking) layer "C" contains colloidal silver particles.
2. After exposure and development:
Partial blue light exposure (B↓) produces silver (shaded area) and silver halide complexes due to action of solvent in developer.
Complexes (Ag+) diffuse into layer "C" and precipitate on silver particles.
Green light (G↓) and red light (R↓) exposures produce metallic silver in appropriate layers as well as silver halide complexes. However, iodine ions released in silver development rapidly diffuse upward to layer "C" and block precipitation of silver halide complexes formed more slowly.
3. After bleaching and fixing:
The dyes in layers B_2, D_2, and E_2 have been bleached in proportion to the developed silver in these and adjacent layers. Additional bleaching of the yellow dye is initiated by silver aggregates in layer "C" formed in blue exposure areas. In practice, a positive silver image is formed in layer "C," which is governed by the relative blue, green, and red light exposure values. This mask image improves color reproduction automatically.

Process Limitations

The main disadvantage of the Cibachrome process is the high acidity of the dye-bleach solution. This is required to achieve the breakdown of the chemically stable azo dyes. In any event, the bleach solution is corrosive and will attack ordinary plumbing materials, such as iron, copper, and concrete. The solution must be neutralized, therefore, before it is discharged into waste lines and sewers. Neutralization is easily secured by adding sodium bicarbonate to used bleach solutions. An ample supply of neutralizing powder is included in each Cibachrome P-12 processing kit.

Suitable materials of construction for Cibachrome processing equipment, solution containers, plumbing, etc., are listed in the table below:

MATERIAL	DEV	BLEACH	FIX	WASH
Aluminum	—	—	—	—
Iron	—	—	—	—
Hastelloy C4	+	O	+	+
Bronze	—	—	—	—
Brass	—	—	—	—
Nickel	—	—	—	—
*Stainless steel AISI 318L	+	+	+	+
Titanium	+	+	+	+
Zinc	—	—	—	—
Copper	—	—	—	—
Plexiglas	+	O	+	+
Epoxy resin with fiberglass	O	—	O	+
Glass	+	+	+	+
Rubber, hard rubber	O	O	O	+

MATERIAL	DEV	BLEACH	FIX	WASH
Neoprene	+	○	+	+
†Nylon (polyamide)	+	−	+	+
Polychlorotrifluoroethylene	+	+	+	+
*Polyethylene	+	+	+	+
*Polypropylene	+	+	+	+
Polyester with fiberglass	○	○	+	+
Polystyrene	+	+	+	+
Teflon (polytetrafluoroethylene)	+	+	+	+
Polyurethane	−	−	−	−
*PVC (polyvinylchloride)	+	+	+	+

*preferred materials
†should not be used for bushings, gears, belts, etc.

+ suitable

○ only partly suitable

− not suitable

Problems may also arise in the printing of color slides that have a very wide density range and/or high contrast. Dodging, burning-in, or masking is required in such instances to prevent loss of detail in the print image. You will find a detailed discussion of this topic and of corrective measures in Chapter 9.

SECTION 2

The Cibachrome Products

CHAPTER 4

Cibachrome Print Materials

Color photographic materials generally must be used under more restricted conditions of exposure and processing than black-and-white films and papers, because the much more complex formation of three interrelated dye images requires a predetermined balance of responses at every step of image formation. This is also true of the different types of Cibachrome materials. Furthermore, while all Cibachrome products are based on the same dye-bleach principle, there are significant differences between specific material-process combinations—especially between the older and newer self-masking systems and between amateur and professional processes.

For example, Cibachrome-A print material is designed for the making of reflection color prints from 35mm slides in sizes up to 16×20 inches, in a home darkroom with one-shot chemicals of Process P-12. Cibachrome-II materials, on the other hand, are intended for the production of a wide variety of prints in professional color laboratories with the replenishable solutions of Process P-3. In the amateur printing system emphasis must be and has been placed on operational simplicity, maximum processing latitude, and rapid access, whereas in the professional process greater emphasis is placed on compatibility with various processing machines, processing uniformity, and minimum chemical costs.

In view of the close relation between product and process design and application, it is best to treat each such system as a unit rather than all sensitized materials in one group and all chemical processes in another. This approach will be used here and the two most prominent systems will be described in detail: the Cibachrome-A home darkroom system and the new professional self-masking system. The older professional products Cibachrome Print Type D-182 and Cibachrome Transparent Type-661 and the associated chemical processes P-10 and P-18 will not be discussed since they are being replaced by the improved system. A tabulation of all these products is given below, however, as a matter of interest.

THE CIBACHROME-A SYSTEM

The two main components of this system are a reflection print material for color

SENSITIZED MATERIAL	CHEMICAL PROCESS	MAIN APPLICATION AND USERS
Cibachrome-A A-182 (Hi-Gloss) & ARC (Pearl)	P-12	Reflection color prints; hobbyists in home darkrooms
Cibachrome Print Type D-182 (Hi-Gloss)	P-10 or P-18	Reflection color prints; professionals in commercial color laboratories
Cibachrome-II Type CRC-895 (Pearl) Type CPS-462 (Brilliant)	P-3	Reflection color prints of improved quality; professionals in commercial color laboratories
Cibachrome Transparent Type D-661	P-10	Duplicate color transparencies for display; professionals in commercial color laboratories
Cibachrome-II Transparent	P-3	Duplicate color transparencies of improved quality; professionals in commercial laboratories

printing from color slides with home darkroom equipment and Process P-12, which is designed for simple processing equipment such as drums or trays, with three chemical solutions for one-shot use over a wide range of temperatures.

The sensitized material is available in 4×5-inch, 8×10-inch, 11×14-inch, and 16×20-inch sizes in quantities ranging from 10 sheets of 16×20-inch to 50 sheets of 8×10-inch material. Each package contains a sealed opaque pouch, which keeps the enclosed sensitized material in the desired environment until use. All sheets in a pouch face the same way with the emulsion toward the label glued onto the pouch.

At present, the material is supplied in two surface types, Hi-Gloss and Pearl, which is a slightly textured luster surface. The Hi-Gloss material (Type A-182) is on a white opaque triacetate film base and the Pearl material (Type ARC) on an RC paper base.

Construction and Important Properties of the Material

The construction of Cibachrome-A material is shown schematically in Figure 25. The image-forming layers are coated on one side of the white opaque base and a matte anti-curl gelatin layer is coated on the other side. This sandwich-type construction provides good flatness before, during, and after processing and thereby facilitates handling during exposure, processing, and print finishing.

Each of the three light-sensitive layers is divided into two components, only one of which contains an appropriately colored image dye. This layer-splitting technique yields improved tone reproduction and higher speed, as illustrated in Figure 26. When only a single layer is used that contains the light-sensitive silver halide crystals and the azo image dye, much actinic light is lost during exposure because of absorption by the dye. For example, blue light that would normally be available for exposure of the blue-sensitive top emulsion is absorbed by the yellow image dye before it can reach unexposed silver halide grains. The resultant loss in speed is quite substantial—about 40×; moreover, tone reproduction is adversely affected, as shown in curve A in Figure 26. When an undyed, blue-sensitive layer is placed on top of the main yellow dyed emulsion, an auxiliary blue-separation image is formed. During the dye-bleaching step this auxiliary silver image causes additional bleaching of the yellow dye in the adjacent main layer by a so-called remote bleaching process. This remote action extends only into the upper strata of the main image layer, however, with the result depicted by curve B in Figure 26. The combination of A and B gives the final sensitometric curve C, which shows the net gain in speed (it is displaced toward the left) and the improvement in tone reproduction (its longer straight-line portion) compared to the single-layer material A.

The emulsion layers are protected against abrasion and other physical abuse by a thin hardened gelatin layer on top. Another auxiliary layer located beneath the blue-sensitive emulsion functions as a yellow filter and prevents any residual blue light from reaching the lower emulsions that have inherent blue sensitivity. The desired absorption of blue light is secured by the use of colloidal silver, that is, metallic silver particles of very small and selected size dispersed in gelatin. These are removed during processing together with the negative image silver.

The multiple-layer assembly also contains a thin gelatin layer between the bottom green-sensitive and the top red-sensitive emulsions. This interlayer traps chemical by-products formed during processing that would cause unwanted inter-image effects.

An unexposed, unprocessed sheet of Cibachrome-A material appears dark brown when viewed in white light from the front or emulsion side and white from the back. The front appearance is the result of the high concentration of yellow colorants and silver halides in the layers near the surface, whereas the back appearance is explained by the strong, non-selective reflectivity of the white opaque film or paper base.

The triacetate film base as well as the RC paper base with its two polyethylene layers on opposite sides of the central paper core absorb only very small amounts of the processing solutions during the normal processing cycle. Consequently, solution carry-over is minimal and total washing and drying times are greatly reduced. These supports also render the print materials moisture-insensitive before and after processing compared to materials on normal paper base.

The triacetate base material is somewhat brittle, however, and should be kept under reasonable conditions of relative humidity (above 30 percent RH). The RC paper base, on the other hand, is apt to delaminate at corners or edges when immersed in water or chemical solutions for prolonged periods of time. Mounting of both types of material will be discussed in Chapter 11.

Photographic Characteristics

The photographic characteristics of Cibachrome-A material are designed for the printing of 35mm or other small-format color slides with simple kinds of enlargers normally used in home darkrooms. The dominant color slide films are Kodachrome and Ektachrome types. Cibachrome-A material is balanced, therefore, to give good gray scale reproduction from these kind of slides. Some adjustments in filter balance are required, however, to compensate for the differences in spectral absorption of different dye sets. A label giving the basic filter recommendations for four different color slide films is attached to each package of Cibachrome-A material.

Speed and Reciprocity Failure

The speed of Cibachrome-A material is that of a typical projection speed product. There is no standard method, however, for determining the speed of color print materials and, therefore, no speed values or exposure indexes are published. Exposure recommendations are given in terms of lens aperture settings—f-stops—and exposure times for a given enlarger type and lamp wattage used at a given image magnification. Alternately, the total required exposure can be specified in terms of foot-candle-seconds for a typical slide. With present Cibachrome-A material this value is about 7.5 foot-candle-seconds. This would translate into an exposure of about 30 seconds at $f/5.6$ for an 8×10-inch print made from a 35mm slide with a condenser enlarger equipped with a 75-watt tungsten enlarger lamp. This kind of setup provides an illuminance of about 0.25 foot-candle at the printing easel on the average.

The effective speed of Cibachrome-A material, like that of all other photographic films and papers, varies with changes in light intensity. The lack of constancy in response is known as reciprocity failure. In practice this means that the effective speed tends to be higher at normal light-intensity levels than at low levels. For example, the correct exposure at a 1 foot-candle level of illumination may be 5 seconds, but at 1/16 foot-candle it may have to be 110 rather than 16×5, or 80, seconds owing to reciprocity failure. Moreover, the different emulsions used in Cibachrome-A print material have somewhat different reciprocity characteristics. Therefore, substantial changes in exposure conditions affect not only the overall speed of the material but also its color balance. These changes in response can be shown in separate graphs, one for changes in speed and one for changes in color balance, or the presentation can be combined in a single table. (A table is easier to interpret and use and is included in the chapter entitled "Exposing Cibachrome Print Material.")

Color Balance

The speed relationship between the blue-, green-, and red-sensitive emulsion layers of a color printing material such as Cibachrome-A determines its color balance. Because of its intended application in the printing of color slides, the color balance of Cibachrome-A material is adjusted, on the average, to provide a neutral reproduction of a gray-scale of a standard color slide when the printing light has a color temperature of about 3200K. Considerable differences in color balance can and do exist, however, between batches of Cibachrome-A print material as a result of manufacturing variations. Such changes in color balance are acceptable in color print materials because the required color balance corrections can be easily obtained through the use of color filters in printing. Moreover, considerable differences in the color quality of printing light exist between enlargers due to differences in lamps, reflectors, filters, lenses, operating voltage, etc., so that even a fixed color balance of the printing material would not allow a uniform filter balance to be used in the field.

It should be noted also that slow changes in speed and color balance occur with aging of the print material, the rate of change depending for the most part on storage temperature. Again, such changes can be offset by appropriate adjustments in exposure and in filter balance and have no effect on final image quality.

Gradation, Contrast Balance and Tone Reproduction

The brightness values of a color print image are the major determinants of image quality. They are controlled primarily by the tone scale of the color slide image and by the tone reproduction characteristics of the print material. The terms "gradation" and "contrast" are often used to describe the overall, macro-tone reproduction characteristics of a photographic material. Cibachrome-A has a soft gradation, or low contrast, compared with negative-to-positive type print materials, because color slides generally have rather high image contrast and a wide density range—properties that are needed in images that are viewed in dark-surround conditions such as prevail during projection in a darkened room. Cibachrome prints are viewed under bright-surround conditions, however, and therefore must have significantly lower contrast than the slides from which they are made.

The overall tone reproduction characteristics of a photographic material can be depicted by means of a sensitometric curve that shows the relation between image exposure and image density. For a trichromatic-type color photographic material three such curves are needed—one for its blue, one for its green, and one for its red densities. A typical set of sensitometric curves for Cibachrome-A material is reproduced in Figure 27. The densities of the dye images can be measured in various ways, but the most meaningful to the end user are integral spectral density values, that is, the total blue, green, and red densities at every point, each the sum of one primary and two secondary absorptions of the three image dyes. You will note that the curves derived in this fashion are nearly coincident and that they have a gradient of about 1.10, which is close to the optimum value for good tone reproduction. In spite of this inherently soft gradation of Cibachrome-A material, highlight detail is often lost when prints are made from contrasty slides. Corrective action such as dodging, burning-in, reduced development, and masking can be used to minimize or prevent such image degradation.

Color Reproduction Quality

Cibachrome-A print images generally are distinguished by having very good color saturation and good hue discrimination. Reds and greens tend to be especially well saturated and modulated. Blues, however, tend to be somewhat dark, and yellows and other pastel colors often are rendered too light. These and other color reproduction problems are due in part to the unwanted secondary absorption characteristics of the dyes in the slide film images and Cibachrome-A material and in part to deficiencies in tone reproduction (see Figure 20). Built-in inter-image effects afford appreciable correction of color reproduction errors but noticeable, and sometimes objectionable, color errors remain in Cibachrome-A reproductions. These can be overcome only by more complete color masking and improved tone reproduction in the highlight region. Both types of improvement have been incorporated in the new self-masked Cibachrome II system. Contrast control in the highlights can be achieved fairly easily, however, with any print by use of a contrast mask.

Granularity, Resolution and Image Sharpness

Cibachrome-A has low granularity, and whatever graininess may be apparent in a print will have been caused by the granularity of the color slide image or the silver mask, if one has been used.

The resolving power and sharpness of Cibachrome-A prints also are very good owing to the low scattering of light within the dye-containing image layers. A resolution of 55 line-pairs per mm is obtained with high-contrast targets, and at 50 percent modulation the resolution is about 17 line-pairs per mm.

Latent-Image Characteristics

Cibachrome-A material has excellent latent-image stability. No perceptible change in image density or color balance occurs even when processing of exposed prints is delayed for several days. Refrigeration of exposed material is not required, but temperatures above 70° to 80°F should be avoided.

Storage and Handling

Unopened packages of Cibachrome-A material will maintain good photographic quality for up to six months when kept below 70°F; exposure to higher temperatures should be avoided. The useful life of the material can be extended to one year at 40°F and two years at 0°F.

The speed, overall color balance, and contrast balance between layers do change slowly, however, with age, and in time color and gray-scale reproduction will become unsatisfactory.

Opened packages of material should be protected from high relative humidity (above 60 percent) and high temperature (above 70°F). If properly stored, opened packages will have about the same useful life as material in original sealed pouches. It is recommended that the print material be kept in its original plastic pouch, which can be folded over after opening. Chemical fumes and dirt can be harmful, and it is best to keep opened packages away from photographic chemicals and out of mixing rooms.

Cibachrome-A print material should be handled in complete darkness. Very dim green safelight illumination is permissible, but the tolerable intensity level is so low as to render such illumination useless except for general orientation within the darkroom. The unprocessed material is susceptible to mechanical and chemical actions resulting from improper, rough handling. Scratches, pressure marks, and fingerprints are the usual manifestations of such abuse. Other artifacts can be caused by discharges of static electricity at the emulsion surface. Such static marks can take the form of light spots or tree-branch patterns, depending on the polarity of the charge. Low relative humidity and abrupt separation of sheets foster the generation of static electricity, but very high relative humidity can also be a problem because gelatin layers tend to stick under such conditions; this promotes contact electrification.

Still other artifacts can be caused by droplets of water or chemical processing solutions that are spilled accidentally on the dry print surface before processing. Water marks can also be encountered when water droplets are permitted to remain on the emulsion surface during print drying.

Occasionally a manufacturing defect will seriously interfere with the quality of a print. Such defects may take the form of colored spots or lines or blotchy marks. Defective material should be returned to the manufacturer for evaluation and replacement. Samples of the defect as well as unexposed sheets should be submitted together with information on the batch number, which is printed on each package label. It is best, in fact, to return the original package whenever possible.

CHAPTER 5

Cibachrome Processing Chemicals

PROCESS P-12

The three chemical solutions of Process P-12 are formulated for use with the two amateur-type Cibachrome-A print materials A-182 (Hi-Gloss) and ARC (Pearl). The working-strength solutions are prepared from proprietary concentrated solutions and one powder packaged in plastic bottles and plastic pouches. The components are supplied in two-quart and five-quart kits as well as in individual units. A two-quart kit is sufficient for processing 20 8 × 10-inch sheets of print material or the equivalent. A Discovery Kit is also available; it contains 20 4 × 5-inch sheets of Cibachrome-A and the solutions for processing.

The three chemical processing solutions are a black-and-white developer, a combination dye and silver bleach, and a fixer.

The working-strength solutions are used once and then discarded. The use of fresh solutions for each print assures greatest simplicity and maximum uniformity of results when simple processing equipment, such as drums and trays, is used at irregular intervals. A quantity of sodium bicarbonate is also supplied in each kit, sufficient for neutralizing all of the spent bleach solution prior to disposal.

The processing steps and recommended treatment times for drum and tray processing are given in the following table. The preferred processing temperature is 75°F but, depending on local conditions, the lower or higher temperatures can be used with equivalent results. Some adjustments in exposure and color filter balance may have to be made, however, from the recommended values.

Presoaking

Presoaking is useful for promoting even development and must be used for 16 × 20-inch prints when processing is done with a drum or trays. It is well to use it for all size prints, however, in the interest of standardizing your operating procedure.

CIBACHROME PROCESS P-12 FOR DRUM OR TRAY PROCESSING
(WITH AND WITHOUT OPTIONAL WATER RINSES)

STEP	FUNCTION	TIME INCLUDING DRAINING		
		68°F±3°F	75°F±3°F	80°F±3°F
1*	Presoaking	1/2 min.	1/2 min.	1/2 min.
2	Developing	2 1/2 min.	2 min.	1 1/2 min.
3*	Rinsing	1/2 min.	1/2 min.	1/2 min.
4	Bleaching	4 1/2 min.	4 min.	3 1/2 min.
5*	Rinsing	1/2 min.	1/2 min.	1/2 min.
6	Fixing	3 1/2 min.	3 min.	2 1/2 min.
7	Washing	3 1/2 min.	3 min.	2 1/2 min.
TOTAL		14 min.	12 min.	10 min.
TOTAL with *optional rinses		15 1/2 min.	13 1/2 min.	11 1/2 min.

Developing

The developer of the P-12 process is a phenidone-hydroquinone-type black-and-white developer of rather conventional formulation. The working-strength solution contains more than the usual amounts of fog inhibitors, however, because even small amounts of fog silver in unexposed areas of the print image would cause an undesirable reduction in maximum density due to the super-proportional action of the bleach.

The developer concentrate is supplied in two parts for maximum shelf life. The ready-to-use solution is well buffered so that small variations in dilution have little effect on speed and contrast. Moreover, variations in developer temperature and in developing time have less than normal effect on tone reproduction because development is carried close to completion and because the gradient of the negative sensitometric curve is very low.

Mixed, ready-to-use developer changes in color on standing from a straw-yellow to a deeper yellow color. This has no effect on developer activity nor does it cause staining of whites. On prolonged exposure to air the developer will turn brown, which is a signal of excessive deterioration. Do not use such an exhausted solution!

Rinsing

A water rinse after development minimizes developer carry-over into the bleach and is especially desirable in tray processing and with drums that do not drain easily. Excessive developer carry-over will cause the generation of excessive amounts of sulfur dioxide gas when the very acid bleach reacts with the sodium sulfite in the developer. This gas has an unpleasant odor and when inhaled can cause severe coughing and even choking in extreme cases. Unless you are bothered by the odor, you will not find the rinsing step necessary with most drums, but as mentioned it is recommended with tray processing where the evolving gas can rise freely from the large solution surface.

Bleaching

The bleach is the most critical and special processing solution of the Cibachrome process. Its main ingredients are the bleach catalyst; a strong acid; and a silver ligand, or complexing agent. Also included are an antioxidant and other chemicals that enhance solubility, activity, wetability, and stability of the concentrated and working-strength solutions. The acid is supplied in powder form for safety reasons and is relatively innocuous until dissolved in water or some other solvent.

The ready-to-use bleach solution is clear and has an orange-brown color and a weak musky odor. The color remains constant on standing but the odor dissipates. The pH of the solution is near 0.8. This means that the solution is strongly acidic and also corrosive to a variety of materials. In a normal darkroom environment, however, it poses no hazards or undue handling problems. In fact, conventional color developing solutions are potentially more troublesome because of their high alkalinity and tendency to cause dermatitis. Nevertheless, recommended precautions should be heeded at all times, especially with respect to the disposal of used bleach solution.

Rinsing

A short rinse in plain water after bleaching serves the same purpose as the rinse after development. It helps to minimize the formation of undesirable sulfur dioxide gas, which would be formed in this instance through the chemical reaction between the acid bleach and the ammonium thiosulfate of the fixer. Excessive bleach carry-over could also interfere with proper fixation because of the precipitation of sulfur and a lowering of the pH.

Fixing

The Cibachrome fixer is a special non-hardening, rapid fixer that is nearly neutral (pH 6.7), unlike the more conventional acid-hardening fixers. The special formulation is required in order to ensure speedy fixation and solution stability in the presence of the highly acidic bleach solution absorbed by the image layers in the preceding processing step. The use of this fixer also provides the proper pH for optimum dye stability in the final print.

The liquid concentrate as well as the working-strength fixer solutions are clear and colorless.

Washing

The final wash in the P-12 process can be quite short—three minutes at 75°F—because the print material has either an acetate film or a resin-coated paper base, neither of which absorbs significant amounts of the processing solutions or byproducts formed during processing. The final wash, however, will be adequate only if fresh water at the proper temperature is supplied to the print surfaces at an adequate rate. This means that the flow of water should be such as to ensure complete replacement of the volume in the drum or wash tray at least once every 45 seconds. Moreover, agitation must be sufficiently vigorous to provide rapid removal of the chemicals diffusing out of the emulsion and back layers.

Incomplete washing will cause staining and/or premature fading of the dye image.

The wash water should be essentially free of metallic and organic impurities, for example, iron and copper and decayed vegetation. The water hardness as a result of its mineral content should be between 60 and 250 parts per million. Very soft water (below 60 ppm) provides inefficient washing and may thereby cause a loss in cyan (reddish blacks) dye density as well as problems with reticulation or frilling. (The loss of cyan density can be reversed by additional washing in soft water or re-washing in normal or hard water.) The salt content of soft water can be increased through addition of magnesium sulfate (Epsom salt) at the rate of about 2 grams per liter. This improves washing efficiency.

Very hard water (above 250 ppm) may cause the formation of a precipitate on the print surfaces, which normally is visible as a white scum or white blotches only after the print has been dried. A final rinse in de-ionized water or water containing a sequestering agent such as EDTA or Calgon often will help to prevent such scum formation.

Mixing of Solutions

The mixing of Cibachrome P-12 processing solutions is simple because all but two of the components are supplied as liquid concentrates and the two powdered chemicals dissolve readily in warm water. Mixing instructions are printed on all labels and contained in instruction sheets packaged with all P-12 kits. These instructions should be followed closely and checked at intervals since small changes are occasionally made that may require modification in mixing, use, or storage practices.

Use clean vessels for mixing and wash them carefully after preparing each solution in order to avoid contamination. It is recommended that rubber gloves be worn when the chemicals are being mixed. The mixing room should be well ventilated and kept free of chemical dust. Spilled solutions should be rinsed or wiped off immediately to prevent crystallization of chemicals on evaporation of the liquid. As with all photographic chemicals, KEEP OUT OF REACH OF CHILDREN!

Your darkroom sink is a good place for chemical mixing since it will be made of photographically inert material, more than likely will be equipped with cold and hot running water, and will be connected to a sewer pipe. *You must remember always, however, that the concentrated as well as the diluted bleach solutions are corrosive and that they must be neutralized before being discharged into the drain.*

The P-12 working-strength solutions can be prepared in different volumes to best suit your working pattern. It will be to your advantage to mix only that amount of solution that you expect to use in one work session or at most during one week. This is so because stock solutions have better keeping quality than the ready-to-use solutions and preparation of the final solutions is very simple and quick.

The following comments on mixing of the three chemical solutions may also be of help.

The P-12 Developer

Cibachrome P-12 developer is supplied in two plastic bottles marked 1A and 1B in black ink. The working-strength solution is obtained by mixing 1 part of A with 1 part of B and 4 parts of plain water. For example, 1 ounce of A + 1 ounce of B + 4 ounces of water = 6 ounces of working-strength developer. The temperature of the water used for mixing should be adjusted to yield the desired final solution temperature—normally 75°F or 24°C. In the summer, when the cold tap-water temperature may exceed 75°F, add a small ice cube to the mixture of A and B, and then add enough tap water to obtain the correct final volume of proper temperature.

The P-12 Bleach

P-12 bleach is prepared from two components, a powder supplied in a sealed pouch marked 2A in red ink and a concentrated solution supplied in a polyethylene bottle marked 2B in red. The powdered chemicals are dissolved first in water of about 125°F; then the concentrate 2B is added slowly and the mixture is stirred thoroughly. Finally, plain water is added to make the proper total volume. The smallest quantity of bleach solution that can be prepared at one time is 32 ounces because an entire pouch must be used as a minimum. This imposes no hardship, however, because the ready-to-use bleach has a much longer shelf life than mixed developer, and a quart of bleach will be used in most instances before the recommended life span has come to an end.

The P-12 Fixer

The P-12 fixer is supplied as a single-solution concentrate in a plastic bottle marked with a blue numeral 3. The working-strength solution is produced by mixing about 2 parts of fixer concentrate with 1 part of plain water. (Instructions for mixing different volumes of working-strength fixer are given on page 43). The concentrated stock solution as well as the working-strength fixer are clear and colorless and will remain so unless contaminated or heated excessively. The ready-to-use solution has the same good keeping quality as the bleach; it is sensible, therefore, to prepare at least one quart of fixer at a time.

Neutralizing Powder

The neutralizing powder normally is not mixed ahead of use but is added to a PVC pail or glass jar of warm water (75°F) at the rate of about 50 grams per liter, or 2 ounces per quart, at the start of a work session. The powder will dissolve readily with moderate stirring.

Depending on the size and number of Cibachrome prints to be made during the printing session, more or less neutralizing solution will be needed. (Data regarding the capacity of this solution are given in the next section.) Mixed, unused neutralizing solution will keep for several months.

Capacity, Life and Storage of P-12 Processing Solutions

Inasmuch as the P-12 processing solutions are designed for one-shot use, the capacity of a given amount of developer, bleach, and fixer is governed only by the size of the Cibachrome prints that are being processed and the design of the processor. The solution volumes required for processing different sizes of prints in a Cibachrome drum, or equivalent, are given in the table below.

SIZE OF CIBACHROME PRINT AND DRUM			
	4×5 IN.	8×10 in.	11×14 in.	16×20 in.
Required solution volume per print	1 oz. 30 ml	3 oz. 90 ml	6 oz. 180 ml	12 oz. 360 ml

The same volumes of solution will suffice for tray processing if flat-bottomed trays of correct size are used, that is, an 8×10-inch tray for an 8×10-inch print. These volumes will be just enough to cover one sheet of Cibachrome print material; therefore, smooth and continuous rocking of the tray will be needed to ensure even and complete processing. When more than one print is processed at a time, the solution volumes will have to be increased in direct multiples of the one-print amounts.

Other print processors may be used provided that they are made of proper, inert materials. Some require considerably larger solution volumes, however, to give even processing and may be impractical for that reason.

The concentrated stock solutions of the Cibachrome P-12 process maintain their activity for about 18 months when stored in the original sealed containers at room temperature (about 70°F). When you purchase a kit or individual components, however, some of the total allowable storage period will have elapsed; therefore, it will be wise to buy only a few months' supply at a time.

Storage in a cool, dark place is advisable. Refrigerated storage would prolong the life of the concentrated solutions but may cause precipitation of chemicals. Such precipitates would have to be redissolved before preparation of the working-strength solution.

Mixed, ready-to-use P-12 processing solutions have the following life span when stored in well-stoppered bottles at room temperature:

DEVELOPER		
full bottle	4 weeks	
partly full	2 weeks	
BLEACH		
full bottle		6 months
partly full		4 months
FIXER		
full or partly		
full bottle		6 months

Glass or polyethylene bottles are recommended for the storage of all P-12 processing solutions. Dark brown bottles offer protection from light and are preferred. Bottle caps should be made of a suitable plastic and provide an airtight seal. Whenever possible, all bottles should be completely filled, especially those containing developer solution.

Disposal of Used Solutions

For safety and ecological reasons it is important to neutralize used Cibachrome processing solutions before they are discharged into a sewer or other waste receptacle. The spent bleach solution is especially in need of neutralization because it is highly acidic and corrosive to materials commonly used in household plumbing. The recommended procedure is to drain the used developer, bleach, and fixer solutions into a PVC pail or other inert container of at least half-gallon capacity that has been half-filled with neutralizing solution. The spent processing solutions are added to the pail in the sequence of the processing schedule.

More specifically, about six ounces of neutralizing solution should be available for one 8×10-inch print or equivalent. Obviously, a 16×20-inch print will require four times as much neutralizing solution. As mentioned, neutralizing powder is supplied in each P-12 kit and is to be dissolved at the rate of about two ounces per quart of water.

The neutralizing container should not be covered during use because carbon dioxide gas is formed when the bleach solution is added to the mixture. This causes the neutralizing solution to fizz and foam as the harmless gas bubbles rise to the surface, but unwanted pressure would build up if the container were closed.

The exhausted neutralizing solution can be safely discharged into any municipal sewer system or private septic tank because it is neutral, non-poisonous, and biodegradable.

Problems and Cautions

The Cibachrome P-12 processing chemicals, like all photographic chemicals, may be harmful if misused. For example, some persons are prone to break out in a rash when their hands come into contact with photographic black-and-white developer solution. Although the P-12 developer components have a very low propensity to cause dermatitis, it is always best to avoid direct contact with this solution. All three chemical solutions must be kept from the eyes and mucuous membranes in the mouth. Of course, none of the solutions should be swallowed. Specific cautions and antidotes are given on all labels and instruction sheets and should be understood and observed.

A more likely source of problems in normal practice is contamination. Even a very small amount of fixer or bleach solution added to the Cibachrome developer will cause significant, objectionable changes in image quality. Similarly, the addition of an appreciable quantity of bleach to the fixer will render the fixer unusable, while minor contamination of this type will generate the malodorous sulfur dioxide gas. For all of these reasons, it is very important to stress cleanliness during all solution-mixing operations, to use separate containers and bottles for all solutions, and to mark them clearly as regards their content and mixing date. Moreover, the darkroom should be well ventilated to avoid the accumulation of noxious fumes.

Misuse and Substitutions

Photographers tend to be experimenters and often attempt to modify procedures recommended by manufacturers. This may take the form of altering prescribed processing times or dilution of chemicals or may lead to attempts to use solutions beyond their rated capacity or life span. Alternately, substitute formulas may be tried or used for a variety of reasons. While it would be wrong and pointless to argue against such experimentation, a strong word of caution is in order because the true value of any non-standard procedure often cannot be judged from a casual appraisal of a few prints.

For instance, there may be serious flaws in the special procedure as regards stability of the dye image, but this deficiency may not become apparent for weeks or even months and years. Take the deliberate shortening of recommended processing times: no apparent change in image quality will result from a decrease in bleaching, fixing, or final washing time, but when any one of these processing steps is reduced significantly, dye stability will be seriously impaired.

The P-12 processing schedule is designed to provide a small safety margin at each step, and extension of processing times beyond the recommended values is quite acceptable within reasonable limits (say, a factor of 2). In fact, it is one of the good features of the Cibachrome P-12 process that it has considerable latitude in the direction of longer-than-recommended treatment times; however, a reduction in time is not safe.

Two other examples may be helpful in pointing up the potential dangers of casual changes in recommended procedures. For instance, the appearance of a Cibachrome print during bleaching would seem to indicate that the chemical reactions have been completed in about one-half the allotted time. The second phase of the recommended period, however, is required for a further transformation of the colorless first-reaction products into soluble compounds that can be removed in the final wash. If the bleaching time is decreased appreciably or if the solution is used beyond its rated capacity, the insoluble intermediate-reaction products will remain in the image layers and will discolor in time to the detriment of print quality.

Similarly, if a conventional acid-hardening fixer is used in place of the P-12 fixer, the pH of the image layers will not be optimum for long-term dye stability. Moreover, the acid fixer is apt to sulfurize and give off excessive amounts of sulfur dioxide gas when the highly acid Cibachrome bleach is carried into the improperly formulated fixer.

The developer is the only solution that can be modified without danger of serious consequences. The changes that can be attained through dilution or substitution are fairly small, however, because a reduction in development leads fairly quickly to veiled highlights, while increased development soon leads to excessive highlight contrast and/or a loss in maximum density. You will find additional information and suggestions on various processing procedures and techniques in Chapters 8 and 9.

In summary, the P-12 processing system was designed to provide a good balance between quality, simplicity, quick access, and latitude. One or the other of these properties is apt to be impaired when an important element of the system is modified; it is advisable, therefore, to proceed with caution and assess the full implications of a change before it is adopted as routine practice.

CIBACHROME-II PRINT MATERIALS AND PROCESS P-3

The new and improved Cibachrome print materials and the associated chemical Process P-3 are intended for use in professional laboratories equipped with automatic processing machines and means for photographic and chemical process control. A distinct Type II amateur process is expected in the near future.

Two reflection-type color-print materials (CRC-895 and CPS-462) and a large-format color duplicating film (Cibachrome-II Transparent) comprise the present sensitized material assortment. Process P-3 is a three-step chemical process that involves development, bleaching, and fixing. Starter and replenisher solutions are supplied in concentrated form for each step. The P-3 processing schedule matches that of the predecessor P-18 process; hence, any processing machine used for P-18 can be converted to the new P-3 process for reflection print material. Changes in agitation and water flow are the main requirements. The most widely used processing machines are of the roller-transport type and wide-width chain-transport units, and process P-3 works well with them. It is also adaptable to leader-type machines and programmed drum processors.

The sensitized materials are available in sheet sizes from 8×10 inches to 30×40 inches, and in roll widths from 3 1/2 to 40 inches (in time, to 50 inches).

The P-3 processing solutions are supplied in various sizes of starter solution and of replenisher solutions, depending on need and specified replenishing rates.

The two main features of the new Cibachrome system are better color and tone reproduction. These improvements are obtained through a self-masking process that depends on chemical interactions between the image-forming layers and a special masking layer. Its functioning can best be explained with the aid of a diagram of the layer arrangement in the new print materials (see Figure 28). As shown in this illustration, the material has nine layers on one side of the white opaque base and a non-curl gelatin layer on the opposite side. The topmost of the nine layers, marked A, is a thin, hardened gelatin layer that protects the image layers from physical damage. Layers B_1 and B_2 are blue-sensitive silver bromide emulsions; B_2 also contains the yellow image dye. The next layer, C, contains colloidal silver particles of such size as to provide absorption of blue light and efficient transmission of green and red light. Thus, the layer functions as a yellow filter during print exposure; during processing, however, it functions as the masking layer.

Layers D_1 and D_2 are green sensitive, while E_1 and E_2 are red-sensitive emulsion layers. All four of these emulsions contain silver bromo-iodide crystals, rather than pure silver bromide crystals, as do emulsions B_1 and B_2. This is a very important difference and vital to the masking effect. Emulsion D_2 contains the magenta image dye and emulsion E_2 the cyan dye. The thin inter-layer I between D_2 and E_1 prevents unwanted chemical coupling of these layers during processing.

The base of the reflection print material CPS-462 is a voided polyester film and that of the material CRC-895 an RC paper base. Both are white opaque, the former because of internal light scattering and the latter because it has a white paper core and white pigmented polyethylene layer. A matted gelatin layer coated on the rear surface of each of these bases minimizes curl of the unprocessed and processed materials. The Cibachrome-II Transparent duplicating film has a transparent polyester base.

The Masking System

Exposure of Cibachrome-II material to blue light and subsequent development in a P-3 developing solution yield the usual negative silver image, split between layers B_1 and B_2. The P-3 developer is unconventional, however, and contains a silver halide solvent that slowly dissolves the unexposed silver bromide crystals in layers B_1 and B_2, while the developing agents reduce the exposed crystals to metallic silver. The silver complexes formed by the "fixing" action of the developer diffuse into layer C and precipitate onto the finely divided silver particles dispersed in that layer. This is akin to the reactions that occur in a diffusion transfer process as used in a Polaroid black-and-white material.

When the exposing light contains green and/or red as well as blue light, layers D_1 and D_2 and/or E_1 and E_2 are affected. As the exposed silver bromo-iodide crystals in the bottom layers are reduced to metallic silver, iodine ions are released. These iodine ions rapidly diffuse upward into layer C and combine with its colloidal silver particles, thereby blocking the precipitation of the silver complexes formed more slowly in the blue-sensitive layers B_1 and B_2.

The net effect of these competing reactions depends on the relative amounts of blue, green, and red exposure at any one image point. To the extent that silver is precipitated in layer C, additional bleaching of the yellow dye will be induced in layer B_2 from below, as indicated in Figure 29.

The system is adjusted to give good gray-scale reproduction when the blue, green, and red exposure portions are effectively equal. This requires an increase in yellow dye concentration of about 20 percent over that utilized in conventional Cibachrome print material in order to compensate for the additional bleaching of yellow dye induced by the low-contrast positive silver mask image formed in layer C. It will be appreciated that this extra yellow dye concentration will remain and contribute to the final color image to the extent that any particular image element contains less blue than a neutral gray. Conversely, yellow dye bleaching will increase with higher relative blue content.

The net result of this automatic, self-masking system is a marked improvement in the reproduction quality of most colors—especially blues, purples, yellows, browns, and greens. Flesh-tone rendition also is better than in non-masked Cibachrome prints.

The tone reproduction capability of Cibachrome-II print materials also is improved, in part because of a more linear relation between exposure and density in the highlight region, in part because of the beneficial effects of better hue discrimination throughout the tone scale. It should be noted, however, that all of the improvements in the new system depend on the proper functioning of complex interactions, with the consequence that some of the latitude of the older process had to be forfeited in order to secure the important gains in image quality. This is particularly true of the development step, which is more critical with respect to time and temperature than the older P-18 development step.

Photographic Properties

The photographic properties of Cibachrome-II materials are similar to those of their predecessor products Cibachrome Print D-182 and Cibachrome Transparent D-661. The new, like the older, materials are balanced for exposure by tungsten light of about 3200K. The average exposure required by the reflection print materials is about 10 foot-candle-seconds, as before (the transparency material has about one-third this sensitivity). Latent-image stability also is very good but reciprocity characteristics are different.

The P-3 Process

The P-3 Process, as mentioned, is designed for use with automatic processing machines equipped with replenishing systems. The working-strength solutions are prepared from packaged solution concentrates. Separate starter and replenisher solutions are supplied in two sizes. The three chemical solutions are a black-and-white developer, a combination dye and silver bleach, and a fixer. The processing schedule is as follows:

STEP AND FUNCTION OF TREATMENT:	TIME IN MINUTES	TEMPERATURE °F	°C
1. Developing	3	86+1	30+1/2
2. Washing	3/4	86+3 1/2	30+2
3. Bleaching	3	86+2	30+1
4. Washing	3/4	86+3 1/2	30+2
5. Fixing (1)	3	86+2	30+1
(2)*	3*	86+2	30+1
6. Washing	4 1/2	86+3 1/2	30+2

*The second period of fixing is required only for the transparency material, which contains considerably more silver than the reflection print materials.

Steps 1 through 3 require total darkness; the remaining steps can be carried out in white light.

Wash tanks 2 and 4 are connected in a forward cascade arrangement (tank 2 to tank 4). The final wash must be divided between two separate tanks connected in a reverse cascade arrangement (second to first tank). Agitation must be comparable to that obtained with roller-transport processors.

Development

The P-3 developer is a phenidone-hydroquinone type developer that contains a potent silver halide solvent required for the masking process. The developer also contains a sequestering agent that has exceptionally high capacity for complexing silver compounds that diffuse into the solution from the sensitized material and would rapidly precipitate and plate out in the absence of this agent. The developer replenisher, when added at the recommended rate (refer to latest instruction sheets for specific amounts) maintains developer activity for long periods of time, provided that the machine throughput is kept above a certain minimum level.

Development is more critical in the P-3 than in other Cibachrome processes because of the interdependence of the masking effect and silver formation in the three different emulsion pairs. The degree of masking varies with development level and hence with developing time, solution temperature, agitation, and chemical activity. The allowable tolerances in these factors are smaller than with other Cibachrome developers for these reasons, but are well within the capabilities of normal processing machines. Of course, other black-and-white developers cannot be used with Cibachrome-II materials.

Working-strength solutions of P-3 developer will keep for about four weeks when protected from aerial oxidation, but fresh replenisher should be made every week.

Bleaching

The P-3 bleach functions like other Cibachrome combination bleaches, that is, dye and silver bleaching occur simultaneously but at different rates. The first phase of the dye-bleach reaction proceeds at a much faster rate than silver bleaching, as it must in a combination bleach of this kind. However, the complete transformation of the dye molecules into soluble amines requires about twice the time of complete silver bleaching.

A unique feature of the P-3 bleach treatment is the triple bleaching action on the yellow dye from above and below the dye-containing layer as well as from within the layer. Proper and uniform functioning of this multiple reaction depends upon good agitation during the initial phases of the bleaching step.

The working-strength bleach solution as well as the bleach replenisher is highly acidic (pH below 0.8), and both must be kept in tanks or other containers that are impervious to sulfuric acid in concentrations of up to 7 percent. The useful life of a mixed bleach solution is about two weeks at room temperature.

Fixing

The P-3 fixer is identical in composition to the older P-18 fixer. It is a nearly neutral (pH 6.7) ammonium thiosulfate formula that is well buffered to withstand contamination by the acid bleach.

The working-strength solution as well as the replenisher has a useful life of more than three months.

Washing

The two intermediate as well as final washes are important processing steps because they have a direct and strong influence on the quality and permanence of the prints, in addition to the stability and cost of processing solutions.

The first wash serves to stop development and minimize developer carry-over into the bleach; thereby it also prevents the generation of sulfur dioxide gas and allows low replenishment of the bleach.

The second wash removes excess bleach solution from the surfaces of the print material and minimizes bleach carry-over into the fixer. It reduces fixer replenishment and also prevents formation of sulfur dioxide gas.

The final wash removes all residual chemical byproducts below levels that would cause image degradation with time. Washing efficiency is influenced by several factors—most notably by water temperature and flow rate, washing time, and agitation. Water hardness also can be of importance and should be above 60 ppm. Very soft water may cause a loss in cyan dye density because of inadequate washing as well as retention of excessive amounts of processing chemicals after normal wash periods.

Drying

Cibachrome-II print materials contain appreciable quantities of water after final washing—especially the color duplicating film, which has much thicker gelatin layers than the reflection print products. Both have gelatin back layers. The presently manufactured CRC and CPS print materials retain about 110 ml of water per m² and Cibachrome-II Transparent more than twice that amount. This water must be removed evenly from front and back layers to prevent excessive curling during drying.

The most efficient dryers are impingement air dryers in which warm, dry air is blown onto the print surfaces at right angles and the moist air withdrawn from the dryer enclosure. The air temperature should not exceed 160°F (70°C). The rate of drying must be controlled to avoid case hardening of the upper surface, which tends to entrap moisture inside the layer stack.

Process Control

Under normal operating conditions process P-3 is stable. The chemical activity of the processing solutions, however, can vary as a result of changes in overall print density, inaccurate replenishment, varying throughput, etc.; it is important, therefore, to monitor the process continuously. For this purpose, pre-exposed processing control strips are supplied by the manufacturer together with processed master strips and recommended tolerance values. The color and gray patches of these control strip images, processed at regular intervals, are measured with a color densitometer, and the data are plotted on a control chart. This provides information on the level of the process at any point in time as well as on process trends, which allows corrective action to be taken before the process goes outside of tolerance limits.

Chemical and physical controls are also employed during solution preparation and machine operation to assure quality and uniformity of results.

SECTION 3

Making a Cibachrome Print

CHAPTER 6

What You Need

Making your first Cibachrome print will be a truly rewarding experience because you will discover how quick and easy it really is to obtain rich saturated colors and sharp definitive detail from your slides. As you gain more knowledge of the characteristics of positive-to-positive printing with this unique material, new horizons of experimental and creative photography will open to you.

Your darkroom facilities need not be large for Cibachrome printing, nor do you need expensive or elaborate equipment. The darkroom itself requires only enough space for your enlarger. Once the Cibachrome print material has been exposed and placed into the processing drum, the lights may be turned on and the processing completed in a separate area; so even a small closet or a section of a bathroom or kitchen may be used quite satisfactorily for the exposure of the print.

Of course, if you presently have a darkroom, either black-and-white or color, you will find that making Cibachrome prints will fit easily into your general routine and that much if not all of your equipment will be usable.

Cibachrome print material must be exposed in COMPLETE DARKNESS. Some who are used to working with safelights may find this a little disconcerting at first, but the time required to take the material from the package, place it on the easel, expose, and place it into the processing drum is usually so short that a safelight is really not necessary. Moreover, the very dim green safelight permitted in Cibachrome printing provides no useful illumination at the working area, and it is not worth the trouble and expense of ordering and installing the special dark-green safelight filter.

A list of the individual items you will need for printing and processing your Cibachrome prints, with some discussion of various types of equipment, is found on page 56.

Equipment for Exposure

Enlarger. Cibachrome prints may be made with any enlarger, either black-and-white or color, that has or will accept color filters; a reasonably efficient lamphouse with a

FOR EXPOSURE	FOR PROCESSING	OPTIONAL
Enlarger	Processing drum, or trays	Enlarging meter
Color filters	Timer*	Roller base
Exposure timer*	Thermometer*	Voltage regulator
Loupe, or magnifying glass (for checking sharpness and cleanliness of slide)	Tray for washing	
Magnifier for focus (for checking sharpness of focus)*		
Easel		
Notebook for records of exposure*		

*If you currently have a darkroom, you probably have all the items marked by an asterisk.

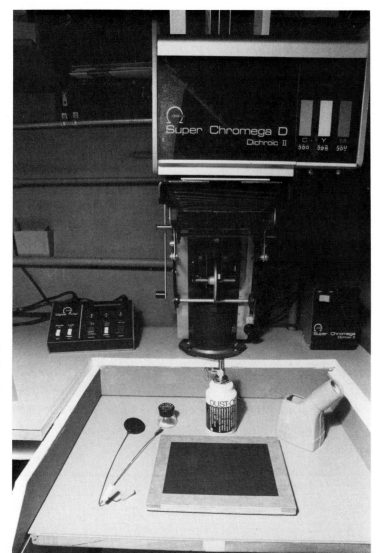

Figure 30. Basic equipment required for exposing Cibachrome prints. In this illustration, a dichroic color head is shown; the filters are built into the enlarger head. In a condenser enlarger, color filters would be required for printing.

75-watt (or preferably higher wattage) lamp; and a heat-absorbing glass or a position for placing such a glass between the lamp and the filters. Most enlargers manufactured during the past several years have been equipped with a "filter drawer" placed between the light source and the film carrier. Your color filters should be placed in this drawer. Of course, all so-called color enlargers have the filters built into the system, and there is no need for additional color filters.

For those having older types of enlargers without filter drawers, the question often arises if filters may be placed below the lens with satisfactory results. As far as color is concerned, your results will be acceptable; but unless the color filters are high-quality, perfectly clean, and placed perpendicular to the lens axis, there can be a significant loss of sharpness and contrast in the final print.

Most older enlargers also lacked a heat-absorbing glass. If your enlarger has neither the filter drawer nor the heat-absorbing glass, order the glass from the manufacturer and place both the glass and the filters above the condensers or directly above the film carrier.

The heat-absorbing glass serves a dual purpose: it reduces the amount of heat from the lamp that reaches the transparency and therefore helps eliminate the bowing or "popping" of the transparency during exposure, and it minimizes distortion and fading of the color filters.

Filters: dyed filters versus dichroic filters. Any quality filter may be used in making Cibachrome prints to obtain beautiful color rendition, regardless of the type or the manufacturer, but now there are two different types from which to choose: dyed gelatin, acetate or polyester filters suitable for use in the filter drawer of the enlarger, and dichroic- or interference-type filters that normally are built into color enlarging heads.

The advantage of the dyed filters is that they can be placed into the filter drawer of a black-and-white enlarger, thus converting it into a color enlarger. The disadvantages of the dyed filters, however, are that they must be carefully handled to avoid fingerprints and dust particles; must be manually changed every time a filter change is required; and, most importantly, will fade with use due to the intense light and heat emitted by the enlarger lamp. Dyed filters, therefore, must be checked from time to time for evidence of fading or filtration will become erratic and often incorrect.

Dichroic filters, on the other hand, are built into the enlarger head, so either small or large filter changes may be made quickly by simply turning a calibrated dial to a fixed number or scale marking. In addition, dichroic filters do not depend upon dyes for color control and are non-fading so that filtration is consistent. You will also find that these filters are more efficient and generally require less exposure than the dyed type.

Enlarger heads: condenser versus diffuser light. Either type of enlarger head will make saturated and sharp enlargements with Cibachrome print material, but there are pros and cons for each.

Proponents of the condenser system will argue that the condenser enlarger will give higher contrast and thereby more "snap" and better image sharpness. It is true that in black-and-white printing, the condenser will give more contrast and snap, but image sharpness will be controlled more by the quality of the enlarging lens than by contrast. In color printing, however, there is virtually no difference in contrast between prints made with condenser- and diffusion-type enlargers.

The condenser system does have an advantage as far as exposing Cibachrome prints is concerned. The efficient concentration of light by condensers often provides as much as a 50 percent reduction in exposure compared to the less efficient diffusion types of light sources.

The condenser system, however, has the distinct disadvantage of enhancing film surface defects, such as scratches and dust particles, that can often spoil an otherwise perfect print. Diffuse illumination, on the other hand, tends to obscure these because the printing light falls onto the film from many directions and the projected images of the defects do not have sharp edges, thus eliminating many retouching problems.

For color printing in general and Cibachrome printing in particular, the use of diffusion-type illumination is strongly recommended for three principal reasons: today most diffusion-type color heads are equipped with dichroic filters, which are more efficient, more consistent, and essentially free from fading problems; diffused light will suppress scratch marks and dust spots and greatly reduce the need for retouching; and most diffusion heads contain quartz halogen lamps as a light source, which offer distinct advantages, as will be discussed later.

Unfortunately, diffusion color heads cost somewhat more than conventional condenser systems; but if your budget will permit it, you will find the extra expense a good investment which will provide dividends in the future.

In summary, either condenser- or diffusion-type enlargers will make fine Cibachrome prints. If you now have a condenser enlarger, use it, but check your filters for fading from time to time and make sure your slides are clean before printing. Compared with a diffusion system, yours may have some disadvantages but you will have the advantage of shorter exposure times or smaller lens apertures.

Light sources. As previously mentioned, for making Cibachrome prints your enlarger should be equipped with a lamp of at least 75 watts in a reasonably efficient lamphouse. For example, with an Omega B600 condenser enlarger and a 75-watt tungsten bulb, an 8×10-inch enlargement from a well exposed slide can be made in 20 seconds at f/5.6. Other enlargers may require more or less exposure, depending upon the efficiency of the lamphouse and the lighting system.

Of course, the higher the wattage of the lamp, the smaller the required print exposure in any particular enlarger. For Cibachrome printing, read your enlarger instructions and use the most powerful lamp the manufacturer recommends for that specific model. Do not exceed the manufacturer's recommendation or you may burn out the system and overheat the transparency because of insufficient means for cooling.

Tungsten light versus quartz halogen light. Most condenser enlargers utilize tungsten lamps as the source of light, whereas most modern diffusion color heads are equipped with quartz halogen lamps.

Depending upon the operating voltage, new tungsten filament enlarger lamps give light having a color temperature of 3059K to 3100K. As the lamp is operated, however, its total output and color temperature decrease gradually due to the blackening of the inside bulb surface and changes in filament thickness. As a result, changes in exposure and filtration will have to be made to compensate for those changes in the intensity and color quality of the light. The color shift will be toward red, requiring the removal of yellow and magenta filters or the addition of bluish-cyan.

Quartz halogen lamps emit light having a color temperature of 3250K to 3275K; unlike tungsten lamps, they maintain this color temperature throughout their life, the light output changing only modestly with age.

The consistency in color temperature and light output of quartz halogen lamps is another reason for choosing a diffusion-type color head if you have a serious interest in color printing.

Many of the so-called "cold light" sources do not emit adequate amounts of blue, green, or red light for normal color printing. The lamp manufacturer should be consulted, therefore, before using any cold light source for Cibachrome printing.

Film carrier. Even though it may seem to be an unimportant part of the enlarging system, the film carrier can play a vital part in printing. Manufacturers offer a variety of types: glass and glassless, single-frame and filmstrip, and numerous other versions in a complete range of sizes.

The glass carrier sandwiches your unmounted slide between two pieces of thin glass. While it has the advantage of keeping the slide perfectly flat during exposure for critical sharpness edge-to-edge, it has the disadvantage of attracting dust or other matter, which can necessitate spotting or other retouching. In addition, you may find it difficult to handle the unmounted slide and place it properly between the glass plates without fingerprinting the transparency.

For 35mm slides, the ideal carrier is the so-called "transparency carrier," which accepts a mounted 35mm slide. With this carrier, you simply place your 2 $\times$ 2-inch mount into a cutout portion and tape the corners to hold it firmly in place. For 2 1/4 $\times$ 2 1/4-inch transparencies and larger sizes, the glassless sandwich-type carrier works well with either single frames or strips.

The question is often asked about printing transparencies in the cardboard mount, versus printing them unmounted or remounting them more permanently. The great majority of slides in cardboard mounts from the film processor are not perfectly flat, but have a rather noticeable "bow" in the center. In printing on any material, if you focus on the center of the frame, the edges can be slightly out of focus, that is, unless you have sufficient light from the lamphouse to stop-down your enlarging lens to f/8 or f/11. Even so, if you want critical edge-to-edge sharpness, you should remount your slides in any one of the numerous brands of slide binders on the market, such as the Gepe brand. These mounts assure you of a flat transparency, as well as protection from dust, scratches, fingerprints, etc. This recommendation may sound as if it is a contradiction of the comments regarding the use of a glass carrier, but putting a transparency into a slide binder is a one-time operation, and once it is mounted it is protected. Additionally, you can handle it by the plastic portion of the binder without ever touching the glass on either side of the transparency.

A word about "Newton rings." When slides are bound between glass, moisture may be trapped inside the mount, causing what is known as "Newton rings" to form on the image. In color printing, these rings will show directly on the print in the form of rainbow-colored circular shapes. There are two ways to help avoid Newton rings: Always purchase "anti-Newton ring" glass or glass binders; and in cleaning the glass or binder prior to mounting the slide, be sure the glass is perfectly dry.

If, in spite of your precautions, you are still troubled with the problem, simply unmount the slide, try to eliminate the moisture, and remount the transparency.

Lens. Last but certainly not least in the discussion of the enlarger is the enlarging lens, a very vital part in the whole chain of photographic reproduction.

Mentioned earlier in the discussion on condenser versus diffusion lighting systems was the fact that *sharpness* is much more a function of the lens than of image contrast. Always remember that the sharpness of your prints will be directly related to the sharpness of your lens. There are many brands of enlarging lenses available, most of them very good in this respect.

In selecting an enlarging lens, try to purchase the very best your budget will permit. It is amusing that a photographer will willingly pay $400 to $500 for a high-quality lens for his camera, but will purchase a $15.95 enlarging lens. Then, when he makes his first print, he wonders where he went wrong.

If you are purchasing a new lens, select one with a maximum aperture of at least f/4, and preferably f/2.8. As a rule of thumb, your enlarging lens will give best overall image sharpness when stopped-down one and one-half to two stops from its maximum aperture, so it will be to your advantage to have as "fast" a lens as practical.

Accessories Related to the Enlarger

Voltage regulator. Those of you who have had experience in making *negative-to-positive* color enlargements are well aware of the effect that voltage changes can have on the final print. Even small variations will change the color of the light sufficiently to cause noticeable color shifts from one print to another.

The great exposure latitude of Cibachrome-A print material, however, overcomes this problem to a large extent. Unless your darkroom is in a location affected by voltage fluctuations of more than $\pm$ 10 volts, there is probably no real need for a voltage regulator in your enlarger system. Minor voltage changes will be virtually unnoticeable in your Cibachrome prints. If you are doing work that requires absolute consistency from print to print, however, a voltage regulator is recommended as an accessory to your enlarger system.

Timer. Today, photographic dealers offer a number of different types of darkroom timers, including the new electronic digital versions with programmable functions. These instruments may be used both for the exposure of your print as well as for programming its processing. Still available, of course, are the standard exposure timers that plug right into the enlarger and are used only for printing.

The type of timer you choose should depend upon your own preferences and to some degree the layout of your darkroom. If you have distinct "dry" and "wet" areas that are separated by some distance, you may prefer one timer for exposure and another for the processing area, to avoid having to disconnect the timer and move it from one area to another. If, on the other hand, your darkroom is compact, a dual-purpose timer could serve both functions.

Loupe. One might consider a loupe, or magnifier, an optional item, but in making enlargements, it becomes a very necessary part of the darkroom arsenal. In the first place, it is very handy in determining the sharpness of the transparency before you take the time to print it. One of the principal virtues of Cibachrome-A print material is its sharpness of detail in the final print, but it does not perform miracles in making a sharp print from an unsharp slide!

The other essential use of the loupe is in checking the cleanliness of the transparency *after* it has been placed in the film carrier and just prior to placing the carrier in the enlarger. Cibachrome-A print material is a positive-to-positive material, and any dust, fingerprints or other foreign matter will print *black* on your enlargement, making spotting and retouching rather difficult. The old saying "Cleanliness is next to godliness" is certainly applicable when making positive-to-positive prints. The Agfa-Lupe is well suited to all your darkroom work and is very modestly priced. Its 8× magnification is sufficient to detect any lack of sharpness or any foreign matter on your transparencies.

Magnifier. Just as a loupe is important to check the sharpness of a slide, it is also valuable to have a magnifier to check the image sharpness on the printing easel. The use of a magnifier eliminates the uncertainty about best-focus position, as the magnification is sufficient to reveal the grain pattern of the slide image for very accurate focusing.

There are a number of models from various manufacturers with magnification ranging from 3× to 25×. For general use, an instrument in the 8×-to-10× magnification range is satisfactory, but you may find an even higher magnification handy in printing from very fine-grain transparencies, such as Kodachrome 25.

Easel. If you presently have a darkroom, you will certainly have some sort of easel with which you are familiar. If not, your photographic dealer can show you many types in various sizes with a number of special features, such as adjustable margin control, adjustable print-size control, and special versions for borderless prints. The easel you purchase should be predicated upon what size prints you may *eventually* plan to make so that you do not have to purchase another in the future.

If you are selecting an easel primarily for work with Cibachrome, again keep in mind that Cibachrome is a positive-to-positive system; therefore, unexposed borders will be *black,* rather than white as in negative-to-positive printing.

The question is sometimes asked as to whether the yellow color of some commercial easels will affect a Cibachrome print because of reflection of the light going through the print material and bouncing back. Tests by some easel manufacturers have shown no effects on the final print from working on a yellow easel; nevertheless, given the choice of a light-colored easel and a black one, the black would be recommended to eliminate one more variable that might affect a print.

Many darkroom workers prefer borderless prints with Cibachrome to get maximum image size and impact. Here is a simple and inexpensive method for making your own borderless easel. Simply cut, or have cut, a piece of 1/2-inch thick plywood to 8 × 10 inches, 11 × 14 inches, or any other usable size. On one side, glue a piece of black cardboard exactly the same size as the plywood, and place strips of double-sided adhesive tape or 3M Post-it Roll #561 on all four edges of the black cardboard. Either of these adhesives will keep the print material flat and in place during exposure. You may put four rubber pads, available at most hardware stores, on the bottom of the board to keep the easel from moving on the baseboard. You will find this home-made easel very convenient and other uses of it will be discussed in succeeding chapters.

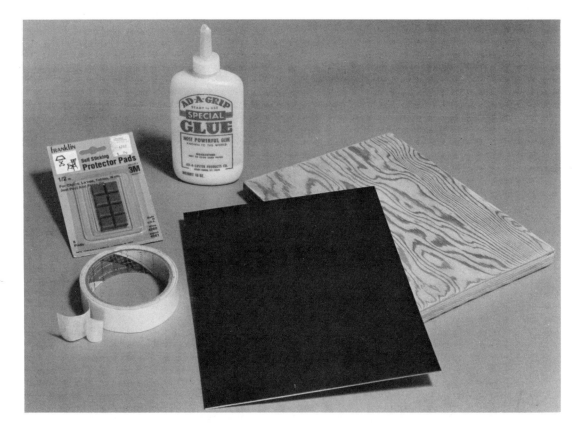

Figure 31. Basic equipment required for making your own borderless easel: plywood cut to desired size, black cardboard cut to same size, glue and double-faced adhesive tape. Rubber pads or some other material to keep easel from moving on baseboard are recommended, but not required.

Notebook for records. By far the simplest and least expensive "accessory" needed in your darkroom is a notebook for recording exposure data of your Cibachrome-A print-making or any other kind you do. Such complete notes will prove to be amazingly valuable in making prints at a later time. You will soon be able to select a transparency, compare it with slides previously made, interpret the data, and make a good print on the first attempt. The importance of keeping the following data on every print you make cannot be over-stressed:

- Date
- Size of print
- Type of slide (that is, Kodachrome, Ektachrome, etc.)
- Name or number of slide, for proper identification
- Batch number of Cibachrome used (from package label)
- Recommended filter pack for type of film used (from package label)
- Magnification reference number (to determine, measure height of lens from the easel, or read from a scale on the enlarger. If your enlarger does not have a scale, glue a cloth or plastic tape measure to the support column.)
- Filter pack used in making the print
- Diaphragm opening of the enlarger lens
- Exposure time
- Manipulation used (that is, dodging, burning-in, masking, etc.)
- Processing notes, if different from standard recommendation
- Evaluation of final print

Optional Accessories

There are a number of minor accessories that may make your life a little easier in the darkroom: a can of compressed air for removing dust from slides, a dodging kit for local manipulation of prints, an anti-static cloth or brush or one of the new anti-static devices that ionize the air above the slide so that dust will not be attracted to the surface.

Enlarging meter. One additional accessory that can be most helpful in exposing Cibachrome print material is an enlarging meter. This device measures the amount of light reaching the print material on the easel and enables you to determine correct exposure from print to print, whether it is from one transparency to another or from one size print to another, without the usual trial-and-error techniques.

Some meters make readings of a small area of the print image, that is, a small spot of the picture area; whereas other meters make integrated readings of all of the light transmitted by the enlarger lens. There are some models that will make both types of readings. There is no question that such an exposure metering device can save you both time and money in all of your darkroom printing.

A word about color analyzers. If you are or have been a negative-to-positive color enthusiast, you may have purchased a color analyzer to assist in the determination of the proper filter pack and exposure in making color prints. If you have a color analyzer, you may wonder if it can be used in making Cibachrome prints. The first answer to this question is that you really do not need an analyzer with color slides; you can get some idea of the balance of the slide simply by holding it up to white light. And after you have made your first test print with Cibachrome and established your own ''correction'' for your enlarger, that correction will be generally applicable to all your transparencies.

Most color analyzers have been calibrated for negative-to-positive printing rather than positive-to-positive; therefore they are not directly suitable for determining the correct filter pack for Cibachrome printing. Some models, however, may be used or recalibrated for positive-to-positive printing. Consult the manufacturer of your particular model for specific instructions.

The color analyzer, however, may be very useful in determining the correct *exposure* for Cibachrome prints in the same manner as you would use an enlarging meter. Follow the directions for your analyzer with regard to *exposure* determination, and it should simplify your selection of the correct f-stop and exposure time.

Equipment for Processing

Equipment necessary for processing of Cibachrome prints is quite simple. Anyone presently having a darkroom for printing will very likely have most of the basic requirements, with the possible exception of a processing drum.

Figure 32. Basic equipment required for processing Cibachrome prints: processing drum, tray, and thermometer; of course, a timer is necessary to maintain proper processing. The stand for the thermometer can be easily made out of plastic or wire, and is a handy gadget for checking the temperature of the solutions.

Processing drum. These drums are light-tight tubes into which the exposed Cibachrome print material is placed so that the processing steps may be done under room-light conditions. There are numerous types and sizes of drums on the market, with sizes ranging from 4×5 inches to 16×20 inches, with one or two models accepting 20×24-inch material. Various brands have different features, but all will enable you to proceed from one processing step to another without opening the drum to light. All work satisfactorily with Cibachrome print material.

The Cibachrome processing drum is excellently designed with these features: a smooth inside surface that permits an even flow of chemistry over the entire face of the print; a reservoir cup that holds the chemistry until the drum is placed in a horizontal position, thus enabling you to pour in one solution while another solution is draining from the bottom; and the capability of being completely disassembled for easy and thorough cleaning and drying.

Trays. Cibachrome print material may be processed in trays, but some of the disadvantages of this method probably outweigh the somewhat lower cost of trays as compared with that of a processing drum. You will need at least one tray, however, for final print washing.

Timer. Timers have been previously discussed. You have many kinds to choose among—from a very simple model, such as the GraLab® unit, to the more sophisticated electronic versions.

Thermometer. One item that every darkroom needs is a good photographic thermometer. Your dealer has a number of models at different price ranges from which to choose. It is suggested that you select one of stainless steel construction, rather than glass, for durability and resistance to breakage.

Miscellaneous accessories. There are a number of other items needed in the darkroom, including mixing vessels, stirring rods, storage bottles for various chemicals, and beakers for measuring and pouring the solutions. One very useful tool is the Pyrex® quart-size measuring pitcher found in most housewares sections of supermarkets or hardware stores; you may want to purchase two or three for mixing and measuring chemicals. These Pyrex® pitchers are among the most useful of all darkroom processing accessories.

Optional Processing Equipment

Motorized roller base. A motorized roller base is not absolutely necessary, but after hand-rolling a Cibachrome or any other drum back and forth for nine minutes each time you make a print, it will become a very convenient and work-saving accessory. A motorized base will free you to do other things while your print is being processed and enable the production of more consistent prints. It is virtually impossible to give uniform agitation print after print when the drum is rolled manually, as there is too much variation in the speed of rotation and the distance covered by each forward-and-backward stroke.

CHAPTER 7

Exposing Cibachrome Print Material

There are a few general considerations that deserve attention before the specific techniques of exposing Cibachrome-A print material are tackled.

First, keep in mind that Cibachrome must be exposed in *complete darkness.* From the time you take a sheet of material from the package, place it on the easel, expose it, and place it into the processing drum, no extraneous light must reach the material! (Tray processing involves two extra steps in total darkness and will be covered in the next chapter.)

Secondly, a beginner may have some difficulties at first in identifying the emulsion side of a sheet of Cibachrome because both of its surfaces are nearly equally smooth. It is particularly difficult to feel any difference in smoothness between the emulsion and the back side of Cibachrome-A Pearl material. There are three ways, however, to identify the emulsion side in the dark:

1. The "Whisper" Test. Rub the tip of your thumb across the corner of each side of the print material while holding it close to your ear. You will hear a "whisper" from the *back* side and no noise from the emulsion side.

2. The "Lip" Test. Since your lips are more sensitive feelers than your fingertips, they can discern the small differences in smoothness, or roughness, between the emulsion and the matted back side of the print material. Slide a corner of each side across your lips. The coarser side will be the *back* side; the smoother, the emulsion side.

3. The "Label" Test. All Cibachrome-A print material is packaged in a light-tight sealed pouch placed inside an envelope or cardboard box. The inner pouch carries a label that contains the following statement, among others: "Open in total darkness only. Emulsion side of material faces this label." So, when in doubt, feel for this label and turn the pouch so that the label faces you. As you withdraw a sheet of material from the pouch held in this position, the *emulsion* side of the material will also face you.

Handling of Cibachrome print material before and after exposure will not cause fingerprints or other markings as long as your hands, especially your fingers, are dry and clean. Normal skin is often moist from perspiration, however, or may be contaminated from contact with processing chemicals. Either condition may cause the formation of stains or markings in the final print image. It is good practice, therefore, to handle the print material only at the edges.

Your first two or three Cibachrome prints may well be the most important, although probably not the most beautiful, prints that you will ever make because they are apt to set your future work pattern. A first test print made from a good standard slide according to recommendations and followed by a second and possibly a third test print made with logical exposure and filter corrections are key steps to a successful start in Cibachrome printing. It is quite natural that a darkroom worker who has seen a few brilliant and sharp Cibachrome prints will want to select his most glowing sunset slide for his first trial print. And in a great number of instances, the first print from a sunset slide can be absolutely spellbinding even when its color and density balance are far from correct. The first elation, however, is likely to turn into great disappointment when subsequent more normal slides produce unacceptable results with the same filter and exposure combination.

It is very important, even imperative if you want to make good Cibachrome prints consistently, that your first test prints be made from a proper *standard* slide that will allow you to properly establish the basic exposure conditions for your enlarger.

What is a good *standard* slide? Ideally it contains the following elements:
• Good flesh tones (avoid suntanned skin)
• Neutral grays
• A range of other colors
• Normal overall density (within one-half stop of correct camera exposure)
• Good sharpness
• A wide density range with detail in highlights, middle tones, and shadows

A good standard slide is reproduced in Figure 33 on page 91. The fair-skinned blond model in front of a patterned gray background holds a Macbeth ColorChecker™ card, which includes a variety of vivid and pastel colors, as well as several steps of a gray scale. A Cibachrome print made from this slide will clearly reveal any deficiencies in overall density, color balance, contrast, and sharpness. The reproduction of the flesh tones, pastels, and grays will depend primarily on correct color balance; the tones of white, gray, and black in the gray scale on proper overall density; the detail in the white sweater and hair on sharpness and tone rendering; and the saturation of the vivid colors on contrast and processing integrity.

Make your selection of a *standard* slide with these factors in mind and use it rather than a spectacular scene for establishing your optimum Cibachrome printing conditions at the very start, as well as anytime thereafter when you need to modify or re-establish your own operating standard.

Let's assume that you have found a suitable standard slide and that you are ready to make your first Cibachrome print. Your two main questions will be these: What color filters shall I use? and What exposure shall I use?

It is not possible to provide exact answers to these two questions without knowing all about your enlarger, your transparency, your processing technique, and the speed and color balance of the Cibachrome print material you are using. Appropriate exposure and color filter recommendations, however, can be given, because there are only a few types of enlargers in general use, slide films usually can be identified with respect to manufacturer and type, and Cibachrome-A material is tested for color balance at the factory and labeled accordingly. Therefore, a simple and usually successful first test can be defined that will help you to establish correct exposure conditions.

As noted above, each batch of Cibachrome-A print material is tested at the factory with a "standard" enlarger and its color balance established for the most popular types of color slide films. This information is printed on a label on each Cibachrome-A package in the following form:

82C1 00-014

Basic filter pack

	Kodachrome	Ektachrome	Agfachrome	Fujichrome
Y	60	60	60	65
M	00	00	00	00
C	15	10	00	10

Your filter pack probably will have to be different from that recommended as a guide by the factory, because the color quality of the printing light can and does vary considerably from one enlarger to another due to differences in lamps, operating voltage, light diffusers and/or condensers, types of color filters, and even enlarging lenses.

Once you have determined your enlarger's "correction" factor, however, it will be a constant until a significant change in exposure condition occurs. For example, if you were to purchase a new enlarger or switch from a condenser lamphouse to a color head, you would have to re-establish your correction factor. Small adjustments in this factor probably will be required occasionally, especially if you use dyed gelatin or plastic filters, which fade with use, or a tungsten filament lamp, which changes in light output and color quality with age, or because another of your enlarger's optical components discolors with time. The most stable conditions and most constant correction factor will be enjoyed by those who use dichroic filters and quartz halogen lamps.

Cibachrome-A print material is balanced on average for exposure by tungsten light of about 3200K color temperature. This means that the relative speeds of its blue, green, and red sensitive layers are adjusted to give correct color rendition when the relative intensities of blue, green, and red light components of the enlarger light are similar to those of a 3200K source. As noted, however, individual batches of Cibachrome material often will depart from this standard balance as indicated by changes in recommended filter packs printed on each package. Moreover, the color quality of the illumination at the printing easel can vary appreciably, as we have seen. Fortunately, it is quite simple to obtain the required blue/green/red light mixture by the use of color correction filters. Of course, the enlarger lamp must not be an exotic type that emits light very different in color quality from 3200K or that is seriously deficient in blue, green, or red content—that is, a daylight-type grid lamp or a mercury vapor lamp.

Another factor to be taken into consideration for optimum color filter balance in Cibachrome printing is the type or brand of color transparency to be reproduced. Different color films such as Kodachrome, Ektachrome, Agfachrome, and Fujichrome contain different types of yellow, magenta, and cyan image dyes. These have somewhat different light absorption properties that affect their color printing characteristics. As a result, different filter packs are required when Cibachrome prints are made from different slide films. The basic filter pack for any number of slides of any given type of film, however, will be the same with any one emulsion batch of Cibachrome print material.

How to Make Your First Cibachrome Print and Establish the Correction for Your Enlarger

As previously noted, on the back side of each package of Cibachrome-A print material is a label on which are printed the basic recommended filter packs for Kodachrome, Ektachrome, Agfachrome, and Fujichrome color transparencies. A typical label would look like this:

82C1 00-014

Basic filter pack

	Kodachrome	Ektachrome	Agfachrome	Fujichrome
Y	60	60	60	65
M	00	00	00	00
C	15	10	00	10

The first numerals and letter "82C1 00-014" identify the product and its batch number; following that is the listing of recommended basic filter packs for four types of transparency film. This table indicates, for example, that under the standard printing conditions used at the factory, a filter pack of Y(ellow)60, M(agenta)00 and C(yan)15 provided correct color reproduction of a properly exposed and processed Kodachrome slide with that batch of material.

When you make your first Cibachrome print, check the label on the back of the package and use the recommendations for the particular type of film you wish to print as a starting point.

Assuming your standard slide is a Kodachrome transparency and that the recommended filter pack printed on your package of Cibachrome-A is Y60 M00 C15, your step-by-step procedure for making the first test print would be as follows:

1. From your set of Cibachrome or other type of color printing filters, select a Y50 and Y10 (or any other two filters that will add to 60), and a C10 and C05, and insert all of them *as well as a UV filter* into the filter drawer of your enlarger. If you have a color head enlarger, simply dial the yellow filter to 60 and the cyan filter to 15, or to other equivalent scale settings that might be suggested in your enlarger instruction manual.

2. After making sure your slide is perfectly clean, insert it into the enlarger and adjust

the magnification for the desired size test print, that is, 4×5 inches or 8×10 inches.

3. Focus the image sharply onto a white sheet of paper of approximately the same thickness as the Cibachrome material. A sheet of double-weight or RC-base black-and-white paper will do for the first print, but subsequently use the back side of a processed Cibachrome print.

4. Make four test exposures on one sheet of Cibachrome material using the "quadrant" exposure mask included in the Cibachrome-A package, or make your own mask out of more substantial cardboard. Figure 34 illustrates how the test exposure should be made.

Figure 34. Use of a quadrant cardboard mask in making the initial Cibachrome test print. The mask should be shifted for each of the four exposures to provide a test print similar to the one shown in Figure 35 on page 91.

Vary the lens aperture setting by one full stop between quadrants. For example, assuming that the wide-open aperture of your enlarger lens is f/3.5, make exposures at f/3.5, f/5.6, f/8, and f/11 with your timer set in accordance with the data given in the following table:

SUGGESTED EXPOSURE TIMES FOR FIRST TEST PRINT FROM A 35MM SLIDE

LAMP WATTAGE	4×5-INCH PRINT	8×10-INCH PRINT
75 watts	12 1/2 seconds	50 seconds
150 watts	9 seconds	35 seconds
250 watts	6 seconds	25 seconds

(Keep in mind that condenser and diffusion-type enlargers differ considerably in light output, so these data can only serve as a guide.)

If you have a light meter calibrated in foot candles, remove the slide from the enlarger, but leave the filters in place. Center the measuring probe of the meter on the easel and adjust the f-stop of the lens until you obtain a reading of 0.25 foot-candle. Replace the slide and set the exposure timer for 30 seconds.

If you cannot obtain a light intensity of 0.25 foot-candle, select another combination of f-stop and exposure time that yields a total exposure (light intensity × time) of 7.5 foot-candle-seconds. Then make a test print in which one quadrant is exposed one f-stop below the assumed correct exposure, one exposure at the correct setting, the third one stop above the correct setting, and the fourth quadrant two stops above the correct setting.

5. Process the print as recommended.

The final print should be similar to Figure 35 on page 91.

Analyzing Your First Print

After processing the print, be sure to let it dry completely before you attempt to evaluate the results, as a wet Cibachrome print will look more magenta-red than when it is completely dry.

It is also very important to view the print under about the same lighting conditions as those in which the print will finally be displayed. Different light sources (for example, tungsten and fluorescent lamps) emit light of different color quality, and this can have a marked effect on the color balance of the print.

In comparing the test print with the original color slide, you should use the same illumination. The best method is to place a white cardboard next to the Cibachrome print and view the transparency by the light reflected from the white surface. Using this technique, you will be able to make a more accurate judgment of the differences in color balance between the print and the slide.

Your first print may very well be off in color balance, but one of the quadrants should have nearly the proper overall density. It is vital that before you start to make color balance corrections you have a quadrant with nearly the correct exposure, since it is very easy to misinterpret overall density deviations as color balance problems.

By viewing a well-exposed quadrant through various combinations of your color printing filters, you will be able to estimate fairly well what kind of change in the filter pack will provide correct color balance, unless the image is so far off in color balance that it is almost monochromatic, that is, all green or all yellow, etc. Normally this will not happen, and you should be within an estimable range from the correct color balance.

In viewing through filters, for example, if a properly exposed quadrant is too blue, it will look more normal when you hold a yellow filter close to your eye. If after study you find that a 20 yellow (Y20) filter gives you the color balance desired, simply add a 20 yellow (Y20) to the filter pack.

The table below will give you some guidance regarding the filter changes necessary for basic color balance corrections:

REQUIRED CHANGE IN FILTER PACK

IF THE PRINT IS TOO:	ADD	OR SUBTRACT
blue	yellow	blue (magenta + cyan)
yellow	blue (magenta + cyan)	yellow
green	magenta	green (yellow + cyan)
magenta	green (yellow + cyan)	magenta
red	cyan	red (yellow + magenta)
cyan	red (yellow + magenta)	cyan

Figure 36 on pages 92–93 is a "ring-around" print guide to assist in evaluating the density and color balance of a finished Cibachrome print.

Correcting the First Filter Pack

Assuming that your first test print has about the desired color balance when viewed through a 20 magenta (M20) filter, your first filter pack (taken from the label of the package) should then be changed as follows:

First filter pack:	Y60	M00	C15
Indicated correction:	___	+M20	___
Resultant sum	Y60	M20	C15

A filter pack, however, should not contain filters of all three colors since this only adds undesirable neutral density that increases the required print exposure. To obtain the correct filter combination, subtract the *smallest* of the three filter numbers from all three values as follows:

	Y60	M20	C15
	−15	−15	−15
Corrected new filter pack:	Y45	M05	C00

To assemble this new filter pack, replace the Y50 and Y10 filters of the first pack with a Y40 and a Y05, and replace the two cyan filters with an M05 filter. (The UV filter remains in the pack at all times.)

When changes in the filter pack are made, an adjustment in exposure may also be necessary. Of course, when you add filter density, you reduce the amount of light transmitted by the filter pack, and by the same token the subtraction of filter density will allow more light to reach the print.

The following table gives approximate percentage changes in exposure for the given changes in yellow, magenta, and cyan filter densities (the same percentage change is made when a given filter is added or subtracted from the pack):

FILTER DENSITY TO BE ADDED (SUBTRACTED)	PRINT EXPOSURE CORRECTION					
	.05	.10	.20	.30	.40	.50
yellow	10%	10%	10%	10%	10%	10%
magenta	20%	30%	50%	70%	90%	110%
cyan	10%	20%	30%	40%	50%	60%

Because of the wide exposure latitude of Cibachrome-A print material, a 10 percent change can be ignored. To illustrate the use of this table, let's reconsider the filter correction involved in the previous test example:

Original factory recommendation:	Y60	M00	C15
Corrected filter pack:	Y45	M05	C00
Required change in exposure (according to table)	−10%	+20%	−25%

Since there are changes in both directions, the net change must be determined as follows: −10% for Y plus −25% for C equals −35%; this is offset by a +20% change incurred with the addition of the M20 filter for a *net change* of −15% (−35+20= −15). The correct exposure for the second print, therefore, would be 15% less than that of the first print, but in practice even this difference would not change the overall print density enough to be really significant in a preliminary test phase.

It should be added that the filter density table is to be used as a guide only, as different types of filters may cause somewhat different effective exposure changes.

The Second Test Print

More than likely, your first test print will have a quadrant from which you can make an evaluation of both the density and color balance. You are then ready to make your second print with the new corrected filter pack and any necessary adjustments in the time setting or lens aperture.

If, however, none of the four quadrants in the first test print has about the correct overall density so that you can estimate with some confidence what the correct exposure will be, you should make a second test print with the same filter pack. Of course, the new test should be made with a much higher or much lower exposure than used initially to make sure that you obtain a properly exposed quadrant from which you can make a reasonable evaluation of color balance. The results of your first test will indicate in which direction the exposure adjustments will have to be made, but keep in mind that Cibachrome-A print material has a lot of latitude, and you must be *bold* in making corrections!

The second or, if necessary, third test print is likely to have about the desired color balance and proper overall density. By then, you will have noticed that the reproduction of grays and flesh tones is particularly critical in a good color print and that any deviations in color balance from correct value are most apparent in these neutral and near-neutral colors.

Determining Your Standard Correction

Earlier in this chapter, there was repeated mention of establishing your enlarger correction and its importance in your ability to make consistently good Cibachrome prints. This correction can be calculated only after you have properly made a test print with corrected color balance.

Assuming you have gone through all of the steps previously outlined and have found that your second print made with the Y40 M05 C00 filter pack (rather than the factory recommended Y60 M00 C15 pack listed on the Cibachrome-A back label) gave you a satisfactory neutral color balance, your correction for the enlarging setup used in exposing that print would be the *+20 magenta* required to correct your first print based upon the factory recommendation. To make sure you fully understand the calculations involved in establishing your correction, the following is a summary of the steps you would have taken:

Factory recommendation: 1st test print too green (required +20 magenta correction)	Y60	M00 +M20	C15
Sum	Y60	M20	C15
Removal of smallest number to prevent neutral density	−15	−15	−15
Final filter pack to obtain corrected color balance	Y45	M05	C00

The key to your obtaining the desired color balance in your second test print was the addition of the +20M filter, so that becomes the correction factor that you use in making additional prints with that batch of Cibachrome-A print material, as well as with all other batches from there on.

For example, suppose the next batch of Cibachrome-A you purchase carries the following factory recommendation for Kodachrome film:

Factory recommendation on label: Apply your correction factor	Y40	M05 +M20	C00
And your correct filter pack for this batch of Cibachrome-A print material will be:	Y40	M25	C00

But suppose you bought a third batch of Cibachrome-A and you wanted to make prints from an Ektachrome slide: simply apply your correction factor to the factory recommended pack for Ektachrome film as follows:

Factory recommendation on label for Ektachrome Apply your correction factor	Y25	M00 +M20	C10
Sum	Y25	M20	C10
Remove the smallest number to prevent neutral density	−10	−10	−10
And your correct filter pack for Ektachrome for that batch of Cibachrome-A will be:	Y15	M10	C00

As previously discussed, your standard correction factor will remain valid as long as there are no basic changes in your equipment or technique. Some adjustments may have to be made, however, to compensate for the color quality caused by an aging tungsten enlarger bulb, fading acetate or polyester filters, or modification of your processing technique.

There are times when you may elect to make deliberate changes in color balance for artistic reasons or to correct an undesirable color cast in one of your transparencies, but none of these conditions should require an involved test such as is needed for the initial calibration of your equipment.

Don't be surprised or confused if your correction factor sometimes will cancel out all filters so that you will use no filters at all (except the UV) in your enlarger. This happens rarely, but when it does occur, don't think something must be wrong!

This extensive discussion of the correct way of determining your correction factor should stress the importance of this first and key step to good and consistent Cibachrome printing. And for many who have already made Cibachrome prints but have had filtration problems, it will be well to go back to the beginning and properly calibrate equipment with a good standard slide.

Once you have properly established your correction factor, have confidence in obtaining the proper color balance for your sunsets, portraits, landscapes, or any other of your favorite slides.

What About Exposure?

Thus far, the discussion has centered on the filtration aspects of a good Cibachrome print, but the need for proper overall print density is equally great in color printing.

Fortunately, Cibachrome-A print material has wide exposure latitude, and an over- or underexposure of even one-half f-stop will not completely spoil most prints. But you want to make perfect prints, not just acceptable ones; therefore, the determination of the correct print exposure is important for quality as well as cost reasons.

Unless you have a light meter for measuring the light intensity at the easel of your enlarger, you are likely to have more difficulty in determining the correct print exposure than the proper filtration. After all, once you have established your filter correction factor, print color balance will be on target for nearly all slides. Print exposure, however, will have to be varied to compensate for differences in overall density of your slide images. You will have learned something about the effects of exposure variations from your first test print in which each quadrant received twice or one-half the exposure of an adjacent quadrant.

It can be a difficult task to estimate what exposure adjustments are required to compensate for an apparent difference in slide density; furthermore, two slides that *look* as though they have about the same overall density may well require rather different print exposures in order to yield the most satisfactory print images.

There are a number of methods for determining print exposure:

1. **Experience.** Exposure estimates based on experience can become reasonably

accurate in time, but are apt to be costly and time-consuming for a beginner. This trial-and-error method can be optimized by systematic testing and good record keeping. A notebook with details on each of the prints you make will become one of the most valuable assets in your darkroom. If properly maintained, you will be able to refer to data about printing a slide of similar subject matter or lighting or even a frame from the same roll of film as the slide you want to print. These data will help you considerably in estimating the required exposure for the new slide.

You will also find it useful to select four slides that vary in overall density in about one-half stop exposure increments from overexposed to underexposed. Make the best possible print from each of these slides and record the print exposure for each. Keep these slides and prints in a reference folder. By comparing any slide that you are about to print for the first time with these reference slides, you should be able to judge fairly accurately what print exposure is likely to give the best results. Remember that a good color print normally must have clean whites and good highlight detail, so compare these areas of your slide images when you decide on the proper print exposure.

2. **An Enlarging Meter.** This is a device for measuring the intensity of light reaching the easel and for determining accurately the print exposures required for varying light intensity resulting from changes in magnification, lens aperture setting, or the density of slides.

As discussed in an earlier chapter, different types of enlarging meters are available from your photo dealer: some are capable of reading fairly large areas, while others permit the measurement of small spots within the projected image of the slide. If your budget permits, it would be wise to purchase a unit that can measure small spots, because you will be able to save time and avoid wasted prints through the intelligent use of such a meter. If you happen to have a color analyzer from past work with negative-to-positive printing, you may use it to determine Cibachrome print exposure.

With either of these instruments, the enlarging meter or a color analyzer, be sure to follow the manufacturer's instruction manual for best results.

3. **A Light Meter.** A light meter calibrated in foot-candles can also be helpful in calculating exposure, as explained earlier in this chapter. The basic exposure would be 30 seconds for a 0.25 foot-candle reading (with the slide removed, but the filters in place).

Exposure Guide for Print Magnification/Reduction

Changes in exposure required for changes in image magnification can be easily determined with any of the instruments mentioned above or by calculation using the factors given in the following chart:

From 4×5 inches	to 8×10 inches 3.2 times the 4×5 exposure	to 11×14 inches 5.8 times the 4×5 exposure	to 16×20 inches 11.6 times the 4×5 exposure
From 8×10 inches	to 4×5 inches 0.31 times the 8×10 exposure	to 11×14 inches 1.8 times the 8×10 exposure	to 16×20 inches 3.6 times the 8×10 exposure
From 11×14 inches	to 4×5 inches 0.17 times the 11×14 exposure	to 8×10 inches 0.56 times the 11×14 exposure	to 16×20 inches 2.0 times the 11×14 exposure
From 16×20 inches	to 4×5 inches 0.09 times the 16×20 exposure	to 8×10 inches 0.28 times the 16×20 exposure	to 11×14 inches 0.5 times the 16×20 exposure

From this table, you can determine how much more or less exposure you must use when changing from one size print to another from the same transparency. The exposure for other degrees of magnification than those listed in this table can be calculated by means of the following formula: light intensity $= (1 + m)^2$. In this formula, "m" is the magnification ratio.

For example, if you project a 35mm slide (which measures roughly 1×1 1/2 inches) to 4×5 inches, the magnification is 4 times (1 inch to 4 inches); when enlarged to 8×10 inches, the magnification is 8 times. The difference in easel illumination between the 4×5-inch and the 8×10-inch images will then be:

$$\frac{(1 + 8)^2}{(1 + 4)^2} = \frac{81}{25} = 3.2 \text{ times}$$

The 8×10-inch print will therefore require 3.2 times more exposure than the 4×5-inch print. Alternately, if you made the 8×10-inch print first and wanted to know the proper exposure of a 4×5-inch print, you would simply invert the figures:

$$\frac{(1 + 4)^2}{(1 + 8)^2} = \frac{25}{81} = 0.31 \text{ times}$$

In this example, the 4×5-inch print will require only about one-third the exposure of the 8×10-inch print.

It is always desirable to maintain the same or nearly the same exposure time and to change the lens aperture to obtain the required change in total exposure in order to avoid problems with reciprocity failure.

Reciprocity Failure

Reciprocity failure, as noted earlier, is a characteristic of all photographic materials and means that these materials fail to maintain the same effective speed at all light levels. Consequently, the formula that *exposure equals light intensity times time* does not hold true if the light intensity is very weak and the exposure time very long or the intensity very high and the exposure time very short (as in electronic flash). In printing practice, this means that with decreasing light intensity in the image plane, the speed of the photographic material also decreases, necessitating a super-proportional increase in exposure time.

Furthermore, in multilayer color materials, such as Cibachrome print material, the different light-sensitive layers do not have exactly the same reciprocity characteristics. Changes in color balance, therefore, occur in addition to the change in effective speed, and appropriate adjustments must be made for both.

In color printing, reciprocity failure becomes most noticeable when the light intensity at the easel is very low because high magnification is used or a very dark slide is being printed. Figure 37 on page 94 illustrates the effects of reciprocity failure.

The following tabulation will give you a guide for making corrections for exposure adjustments in making Cibachrome-A enlargements. In working with this chart, keep in mind that for exposures of less than 60 seconds, there is very little reciprocity effect.

EXPOSURE CORRECTION

FROM ORIGINAL EXPOSURE	TO CALCULATED EXPOSURE TIME				
	40 sec.	*60 sec.*	*80 sec.*	*100 sec.*	*200 sec.*
20 seconds	1.1×	1.2×	1.5×	1.8×	2.8×
40 seconds		1.1×	1.5×	2.0×	2.5×
60 seconds			1.1×	1.3×	2.0×

The chart shows only 20-, 40-, and 60-second "original exposures," and selected "calculated exposure times" from 40 seconds through 200 seconds. Intermediate times in each category can be interpolated.

To determine the *true* exposure time required for an enlargement, multiply the calculated time by the correction factor.

Example: Assume that you have made an 8 × 10-inch print at f/3.5 with a 20-second exposure, and now you want to make a 16 × 20-inch enlargement from the same transparency. Further assume that there were no time corrections necessary in shifting from the batch of 8 × 10-inch material to the 16 × 20-inch material.

From the magnification chart on page 77, you will find that the enlargement from an 8 × 10-inch print to a 16 × 20-inch print will require 3.6 times the original exposure of 20 seconds, or a total of 72 seconds. That is your calculated exposure time.

In checking the exposure correction, you will find that you must use an exposure time of 100 seconds for the 16 × 20-inch enlargement (interpolation between 60 and 80 seconds gives a correction factor of 1.4 and 1.4 × 72 = 100).

The reciprocity failure characteristics of any given material can vary somewhat from batch to batch, especially if the batch numbers are far apart, because of raw material changes that have an influence on this photographic property.

In reciprocity failure, filter corrections must also be taken into consideration. Following is a tabulation to be used as a guide in making filter adjustments:

FILTER CORRECTION

FROM ORIGINAL EXPOSURE TIME	TO CALCULATED EXPOSURE TIME				
	40 sec.	*60 sec.*	*80 sec.*	*100 sec.*	*200 sec.*
20 seconds	—	−C5	−C5	+Y5,−C5	+Y10,−C10
40 seconds		—	−C5	+Y5,−C5	+Y5, −C10
60 seconds			—	−C5	+Y5, −C10

To adjust your filter pack for magnification, use the chart above as follows: From your 20-second exposure for the 8×10-inch print to the 100 seconds required for the 16× 20-inch enlargement, you will see you need to adjust your filter pack by adding Y5 and subtracting C5.

Latent-Image Stability

The change in the latent image on Cibachrome-A between exposure and development is so slight it can be measured only under laboratory conditions. For all practical purposes, it can be ignored.

CHAPTER 8

Processing Cibachrome Print Material

The processing of Cibachrome is simpler than that of any other color printing method available to the darkroom hobbyist today, because of its great latitude with respect to solution temperatures and treatment times, as well as the small number of steps. You will be amazed when you process your first print to see how quick and easy the whole process really is and how simple it is to follow the instructions.

A technical explanation of each of the components of the processing system has been given in the section headed "The Cibachrome Products," as well as a general outline of the steps involved; in this chapter, the discussion is centered on recommended practical procedures, including some variations that can be useful in getting the best out of certain types of slides or in achieving unusual effects.

It is almost inevitable that many darkroom workers will want to develop their own techniques and even experiment with substitute chemical formulae. The hazards of substituting have been delineated on pages 45–46 in Chapter 5, but an additional word of caution is in order: do not start "playing around" with the Cibachrome process until you have mastered the procedures recommended by the manufacturer, that is, if you really want to learn how to make good Cibachrome prints. If you must experiment, learn the basics first so that you will have a good standard by which to measure the true value of your variations. Alternate techniques, as well as the pros and cons of substitution of chemical solutions, are considered in subsequent sections of this chapter.

Choice of Processing Method

A light-tight processing drum unquestionably is the easiest and most foolproof device for processing Cibachrome prints in a home darkroom; yet, there are some who prefer tray processing for a number of reasons. Either method gives good results when carried out properly, and the choice, therefore, is clearly yours to make. Both methods are described in the following paragraphs.

The use of a simple processing drum offers these distinct advantages:

1. There is white light operation throughout the processing period.
2. Your own contact with the chemicals is minimal.
3. The wet, delicate emulsion of the print is protected from handling.
4. Little manual labor is involved when a motor base is used for agitation.
5. Solution temperatures remain more stable inside the drum.

The major disadvantages of drum processing are as follows:

1. One or only a few prints can be processed at one time.
2. Processing consistency is not as easily attained by manually rolling the drum. (A motor base can help solve this problem.)
3. Dividers inside some types of drums to accept multiple prints can cause uneven agitation, resulting in image mottle or streaks.

Tray processing, on the other hand, has the following advantages:

1. Little or no investment is needed since standard photographic processing trays can be used.
2. A number of prints can be processed at a time with relative ease and uniformity.
3. There is good consistency between batches if a standardized procedure is followed at all times.

The chief problems with tray processing are these:

1. Processing must be carried out in total darkness midway through the bleaching step (about five minutes with no light).
2. At least three trays must be used: one for the developer, one for a water rinse, and one for the bleach solution.
3. The temperature of these three solutions is apt to drift excessively during the dark period because of the large solution surface area. (A tempered water bath or good room temperature control is desirable.)
4. The delicate, wet emulsion surfaces are easily damaged when more than one print is processed at a time.
5. Rubber gloves should be worn, which complicates print handling.

Drum Processing

When a sheet of Cibachrome print material is formed into a cylinder and inserted into a processing drum, it will fit smoothly and snugly against the inside wall of the drum because of the stiffness of the print material base. It will be obvious that the emulsion surface of the print must face inward so that the processing solutions will have ready access to all portions of the image. If the print is placed in the drum "backwards" with the emulsion against the wall of the drum, very uneven and unsatisfactory processing will occur because the emulsion of the print will be in loose contact with the drum walls and the action of the processing solutions will be impeded.

Once an exposed Cibachrome print has been placed inside the drum and the end caps put into place, room lights may be turned on so that all processing can be carried out with great ease.

One word of caution: if you use a drum with two removable end caps, be sure to put the bottom cap on the drum *before you expose your print.* Otherwise, you may discover when the lights are turned on after the exposure has been made (the material having been inserted in the drum and the top put into place) that the other end was open! Of course, the print will have been ruined by the resulting white-light exposure.

At the end of the processing steps, you must also be careful in removing the caps so that the bottom of the cup will not scrape the print. This is especially true with drums having "reservoir cups." With a drum such as the Cibachrome drum Mark II, it is recommended, therefore, that the bottom (drain) cap be removed first because it has no protuberance. If the top cap with attached reservoir cup is removed first, make sure you lift the cap *straight up* to avoid touching the print with the bottom rim of the cup.

There are a number of reasonably priced processing drums available at your photo dealer. You will find the modest investment well worthwhile for Cibachrome (as well as other color print) processing.

Many drums are designed to permit multiple-print processing. The Cibachrome Mark II 11×14-inch tube, for example, is actually over 16 inches long and will accept two 8 ×10-inch prints. Other brands have various arrangements for accommodating a variety of sizes.

Processing drums may be easily hand-rolled back and forth on a level surface, but you will find a motorized roller base to be a very handy accessory. Instead of having to roll the drum by hand throughout the nine-minute chemical processing cycle, you simply place it on the roller base; you are free to do other chores while the print is being evenly processed. In addition, use of a motor base will aid in obtaining more consistent results than the hand-rolling technique, because it is almost impossible to develop a truly repeatable pattern for hand-rolling the drum.

Tray Processing

The tray method, as mentioned, has several advantages but requires total darkness during the developing, rinsing, and one-half of the bleaching steps. Fixing and washing may be done in normal room lighting.

Others factors to keep in mind in tray processing are as follows:

1. Unless you can maintain the air temperature of your darkroom at approximately 75°F, the solutions in the open trays are apt to change too rapidly, and you will need a water bath to maintain the required temperature tolerances.

2. You must set up at least three trays containing developer, rinse water, and bleach prior to starting the procedure.

3. You must rinse between the developing and bleaching steps and between the bleaching and fixing steps. As mentioned previously, carry-over of developer into the bleach solution and of bleach into the fixer causes the formation of sulfur dioxide gas, which has a very unpleasant odor and may cause coughing. (In a closed drum, the diffusion of the gas into the atmosphere is inhibited, and many workers find it unnecessary to use intermediate rinses. In tray processing, however, the presence of the gas will be very evident unless you use the in-between rinses.)

4. Rubber gloves must be worn in tray processing.

A problem that may arise in processing a single print in a tray is inadequate coverage because so little solution is required. For example, only three ounces of each solution are needed to process an 8×10-inch print, but that amount is barely enough to cover the print even when the tray has a perfectly smooth and level surface. Trays with molded ridges or depressions in the bottom will make uniform coverage and processing even more difficult unless greater solution volumes are used. It must be emphasized that an uninterrupted and adequate supply of chemistry at all points of the print surface is a prerequisite to uniform image formation. It is impossible to make certain that this requirement is met when tray-processing in the dark with a marginal quantity of solution. This can be particularly tricky in the first step because surface tension can cause uneven wetting of the emulsion and a consequent discontinuity in the critical onset of development. For this reason, presoaking of the print is imperative in tray processing.

Preparation of Working-Strength Solutions

As discussed previously, there are only three chemical solutions required for processing Cibachrome-A print material: developer, bleach, and fixer. These chemicals are available in Cibachrome P-12 kits in two-quart and five-quart sizes and also as individual components through some Cibachrome dealers.

P-12 developer is supplied in two liquid parts: developer 1A and developer 1B, each in a plastic bottle color-coded in black. You should mix only the amount of P-12 developer that you expect to use in a single darkroom session, or over a two-to-three-day work period, as the shelf life of mixed developer is more limited than that of the concentrates: four weeks in a well-stoppered full bottle and only two weeks in a partially filled bottle. Freshly mixed developer is light yellow in color, but the color darkens with age. A dark yellow does not indicate impaired developing strength, but if the solution has a coffee-brown color, do not use it.

According to the manufacturer's instructions, the proper procedure for mixing developer P-12 is shown in the table at the top of page 84.

The packaged P-12 bleach consists of one plastic pouch containing an off-white-colored powder and one plastic bottle containing an orange-colored liquid. The pouch is marked 2A and the bottle 2B, both color-coded in red. Because the contents of an entire pouch must be mixed at one time, the minimum volume of a mix will be 32 ounces. This

TO MAKE	3 OZ.	6 OZ.	12 OZ.	32 OZ.	64 OZ.
Mix developer 1A	15 ml	30 ml	60 ml	160 ml (5.4 oz.)	320 ml (10.8 oz.)
With developer 1B	15 ml	30 ml	60 ml	160 ml (5.4 oz.)	320 ml (10.8 oz.)
Add water at 75°F	60 ml	120 ml	240 ml	626 ml (21 oz.)	1252 ml (42.5 oz.)
To make final quantity	90 ml (3 oz.)	180 ml (6 oz.)	360 ml (12 oz.)	946 ml (32 oz.)	1892 ml (64 oz.)

presents no problem as a rule because the shelf life of the mixed solution is from four to six months.

According to the manufacturer's instructions, the procedure for mixing bleach P-12 is as follows:

TO MAKE	32 OZ.	64 OZ.	96 OZ.	128 OZ.
Start with water at 100–125°F	24 oz.	48 oz.	72 oz.	96 oz.
Add bleach 2A and dissolve	1 bag	2 bags	3 bags	4 bags
Add bleach 2B and stir	100 ml (3.4 oz.)	200 ml (6.8 oz.)	300 ml (10.1 oz.)	400 ml (13.5 oz.)
Add water to make final quantity	32 oz.	64 oz.	96 oz.	128 oz.

Note: In dissolving part 2A, the warmer the water, up to 125°F, the faster the powder will dissolve; however, be sure to cool the solution to 75°F before using.

Figure 38. A simple procedure for mixing bleach part 2A is as follows: Use two Pyrex™ one-quart mixing pitchers (available at most housewares departments). In one pitcher, pour the entire contents of the bag of bleach part 2A and then add about 16–18 ounces of hot water. Stir vigorously until as much of the powder dissolves as possible. In the other pitcher, place 3 or 4 ice cubes, and carefully pour the liquid from the first pitcher over the ice. There will be undissolved powder remaining in the first pitcher; add another 10 ounces of hot water to it and completely dissolve all the powder. When dissolved, pour into the second pitcher and add 100 ml of bleach part 2B. This should give you approximately 32 ounces of mixed bleach, cooled by the ice to approximately the 75°F working temperature. (If the amount does not equal 32 ounces, add sufficient cold water until it does.) Note the use of rubber gloves in mixing the chemicals.

As noted previously, the P-12 bleach is quite a strong acid and must be neutralized before disposal to avoid corrosion of household plumbing. Each kit of Cibachrome P-12 chemicals, regardless of size, contains bleach neutralizing powder packaged in a plastic bag color-coded green.

According to the manufacturer's instructions, the procedure for mixing the neutralizing powder is as follows:

PRINT SIZE	4×5 INCHES	8×10 INCHES	11×14 INCHES	16×20 INCHES
Neutralizing powder per print	1 teaspoon (5 grams)	2 teaspoons (10 grams)	4 teaspoons (20 grams)	4 heaping teaspoons (40 grams)
Added to water	3 oz.	6 oz.	9 oz.	9 oz.

Notes:

1. If neutralizing materials are consumed or misplaced, use regular bicarbonate of soda in the amounts shown above.

2. The procedure for using the neutralizing solution is as follows: place the required amount of neutralizing powder and water into a polyethylene pail or bucket of at least one-half gallon capacity. *After each processing step,* pour the spent developer, bleach, and fixer (in order of use) into the container.

Do not cover the container. The solution will fizz and foam after the bleach has been added. When all three solutions have been mixed and the fizzing stops, pour the contents of the container into the drain.

Figure 39. It is important to follow the directions when neutralizing the Cibachrome bleach before disposal down the drain. After all three solutions (developer, bleach, and fix) have been added to the water with the Cibachrome neutralizing powder, the fizzing of the chemicals will stop, and it is ready for disposal.

Cibachrome P-12 fixer 3 is packaged as a clear liquid in a plastic bottle color-coded in blue. Mixing fixer in 32-ounce quantities will be convenient, and the shelf life is four to six months. Prior to mixing the fixer, shake the bottle vigorously and stir well when mixed with water to obtain even distribution.

According to the manufacturer's instructions, the procedure for mixing fixer P-12 is as follows:

TO MAKE	32 OZ.	64 OZ.	96 OZ.	128 OZ.
Add fixer 3	20 1/2 oz.	41 oz.	61 1/2 oz.	82 oz.
To water at 75°F	11 1/2 oz.	23 oz.	34 1/2 oz.	46 oz.
To make final quantity	32 oz.	64 oz.	96 oz.	128 oz.

Important Cautions

1. Read and follow all cautions carefully before mixing any and all of the Cibachrome P-12 chemicals.

2. As with all household and photographic chemicals, KEEP OUT OF REACH OF CHILDREN.

3. Use clean rubber gloves in mixing all chemicals or whenever chemicals can come in contact with the skin.

4. In mixing the chemicals, be sure to follow all directions carefully, as errors can cause various faults in final prints.

5. Use clean containers for mixing, and be sure to wash thoroughly after use to avoid contamination.

Processing Schedule and Tolerances

As mentioned in the section on Cibachrome products, the volumes of chemistry required for processing different-size Cibachrome prints is as follows:

PRINT SIZE	4×5 INCHES	8×10 INCHES	11×14 INCHES	16×20 INCHES
P-12 chemistry required per print	1 oz. (29 ml)	3 oz. (90 ml)	6 oz. (180 ml)	12 oz. (360 ml)

According to the manufacturer's instructions, the recommended temperatures and times for processing Cibachrome-A in either a processing drum or trays are as follows:

	68°F±3°F (20°C±1 1/2°C)	75°F±3°F (24°C±1 1/2°C)	82°F±3°F (28°C±1 1/2°C)
Develop	2 1/2 min.*	2 min.*	1 1/2 min*
Bleach	4 1/2 min.*	4 min.*	3 1/2 min.*
Fix	3 1/2 min.	3 min.	2 1/2 min.
Wash	3 1/2 min.	3 min.	2 1/2 min.
Total time	14 min.	12 min.	10 min.

*If processing in trays, the developing step and at least one-half the bleaching step must be done in TOTAL DARKNESS.

Experience has shown that a somewhat altered procedure will minimize a number of potential problems and give more consistent results:

1. Presoak the print in plain water at the selected temperature for approximately 30 seconds. For example, if you plan to use the standard 12-minute process at 75°F, presoak your print in 75°F water. Presoaking is mandatory for processing 16×20-inch prints, but is recommended as a standard procedure for all print sizes, especially since it promotes rapid and even action of the developer.

2. Develop with Cibachrome P-12 developer in accordance with the standard time-temperature schedule.

3. Bleach in Cibachrome P-12 bleach as recommended.

4. Rinse with plain water at the selected temperature for approximately 30 seconds. This rinse will prevent excessive carry-over of bleach, and this ensures efficient fixation; moreover, it prevents the unpleasant sulfur dioxide odor.

5. Fix in Cibachrome P-12 fixer as recommended.

6. Wash in plain running water at the selected temperature as recommended.

7. Dry the print as discussed later in this chapter.

This revised procedure requires about one more minute than the "official" procedure, but the benefits will be well worth the extra time. You will remember that a rinse between developing and bleaching is optional for drum processing, but mandatory for tray processing if the unpleasant effects of the sulfur dioxide gas are to be avoided.

The recommended step-by-step procedure for processing Cibachrome-A prints is as follows:

IN PROCESSING DRUM	IN TRAYS
1. Pre-soak approximately 30 seconds at selected process temperature.	1. Same as with drum processing, but in total darkness.
2. Develop for recommended time; for example, 2 minutes at 75°F. Start draining the developer into the neutralizing bucket 15 seconds prior to the end of the developing period.	2. Same as with drum processing, but in total darkness. Spent developer may be poured into the neutralizing bucket later when lights are turned on.
3. Optional rinse for 30 seconds in plain water of proper temperature. (Recommended if odor is objectionable.)	3. Rinse between developer and bleach is mandatory because of open trays. Must be in total darkness.
4. Bleach for recommended time, i.e., 4 minutes at 75°F. Start draining the bleach into neutralizing bucket 15 seconds before end of the period.	4. Same as with drum processing, but first 2 minutes must be in total darkness. The remainder of the step may be completed with lights on. Pour spent developer and bleach into neutralizing bucket.
5. Rinse for 30 seconds in plain water at proper temperature.	5. Rinse between bleach and fix is mandatory to prevent odor.
6. Fix for the full recommended time at chosen temperature. Drain spent fixer solution into neutralizing bucket.	6. Same as with drum processing.

IN PROCESSING DRUM	IN TRAYS
7. Carefully remove the print from drum and wash in running water in a tray for recommended time at the same temperature used for processing. Flow of water should be sufficient to assure a complete change of water in tray content every 45 seconds.	7. Same as with drum processing.

The drum processing technique is obviously quite simple and will quickly become routine. By following the instructions, you will obtain well-processed prints time after time.

In tray processing, you will have to exercise care in handling your prints. In addition to the directions previously outlined, follow these helpful hints:

1. In developing, agitate the solution evenly back and forth over the print. Keep the developer moving constantly by alternately raising and lowering each of the four sides of the tray.

2. In processing more than one print at a time, add chemicals in proportion to the number of prints you are making: each 8×10-inch print requires three ounces of chemistry, so if you are processing three prints, use nine ounces of chemistry. This is required in order to obtain sufficient chemical activity as well as adequate coverage of the several prints.

3. When processing multiple prints, keep all but the top print *face-down* in the tray to prevent one print from scratching the emulsion surface of another. The technique is as follows: Immerse the first print face-up and keep it below the solution surface for ten seconds to make sure it is evenly wetted with developer, then turn it face down. Follow the same procedure with the succeeding prints until all are in the tray. Then begin inter-leafing the prints, bringing the print on the bottom to the top. It is important that each of the prints gets the same treatment in each solution; therefore, you must remove the prints after each step in the same order and at the same time interval as used at the start of the cycle. It is helpful to identify the first print by clipping a tiny section of a corner.

Tray processing of multiple prints is not easy, and it is recommended you try it only after you have mastered the handling of a single print. Then gradually increase the number of prints processed at a time.

A question is sometimes raised regarding the advisability of processing multiple prints one at a time instead of doing them all in one batch. For example, instead of using just enough solution for one print, a larger volume would be placed into each tray proportionate with the number of prints to be processed during an evening's printing session, that is, 18 ounces for six 8×10-inch prints. Then the prints would be handled one by one through the processing steps.

This procedure simplifies and speeds up solution handling, but makes it more difficult to ensure uniform results because of likely changes in developer activity and probable variations in solution temperatures. The developer changes will manifest themselves as a gradual increase in overall image density and a shift in color balance toward yellow as you proceed from the first print through the last. These changes can be offset to a large extent by increasing developing time with each succeeding print by about five to ten seconds, provided the total darkroom session does not exceed an hour or so. If the temperature of the solutions varies beyond allowed tolerance limits, appropriate compensation in treatment times should be made in each session. In summary, this procedure offers some advantages, but has potential drawbacks that should not be ignored.

Temperature Control

One of the main advantages of the Cibachrome process is its great latitude with respect to processing solution temperatures. This applies not only to permissible variations from the selected standard temperature, but also allowable variation in the standard temperature itself. For example, at the preferred standard temperature level of 75°F, variations of ± 3°F are acceptable for each processing solution. This makes it easy under normal circumstances to stay within the recommended tolerance limits when all solutions are adjusted to 75°F at the start of the processing run.

In the winter or summer months, however, it may be difficult in some regions to maintain 75°F, because the darkroom temperature is considerably below or above that value or the tap water is not within the tolerances. In such instances, it is best to adopt a different standard temperature and to make the recommended adjustments in processing times as given in the processing schedule on page 86. You should not allow the temperature of the processing solutions, including the final wash water, to vary from one another by more than 5°F, since sudden and/or large changes in temperature can cause trouble with reticulation of the gelatin layers.

Maintaining the temperature of the running water during the final wash period can be a problem when cold and hot water must be mixed without the aid of a reliable temperature-mixing unit. If you should have this kind of problem, you would be better off using four separate one-minute washes in a tray filled with tempered fresh water after each interval. The print should be agitated frequently throughout the four-minute wash period to promote diffusion of the residual chemicals out of the emulsion layers; otherwise, this is a very satisfactory alternate washing technique and one that also saves water.

Reticulation

Reticulation is caused by a disruption of the normally homogenous structure of a gelatin layer as a result of excessive physical stress as incurred during an abrupt change in temperature. Under magnification a reticulated emulsion layer often looks like cracked, dried mud, or a chicken-wire fence; but if reticulation occurs in one of the lower layers of an emulsion stack, it may impart a satin-like appearance to the print surface after drying.

Reticulation is also apt to be a problem whenever the wash water is very soft (less than 60 ppm) because gelatin layers swell much more in solutions that have a low salt content than in those that contain a reasonable amount of salts. Wash water may be soft because the local water supply is low in mineral content or because a water softener is used. In the latter case, it may be necessary to inactivate the water softener unit during the print-washing period. If the incoming water is too soft, Epsom salt (magnesium sulfate) may be added at the rate of about one-fifth of a gram per liter of water to achieve a better hardness level. You can add the Epsom salt directly to the water in the required low concentration, or you can prepare a stock solution by dissolving one level teaspoon of Epsom salt (about 1/2 oz.) in a gallon of water and then mixing about 12 ounces of the stock solution with a gallon of water for final use. You would use the hardened water in a tray for four successive one-minute washes, as explained previously.

It is not necessary to use hard water in mixing developer, bleach, or fixer solutions because some of the chemicals in these solutions provide adequate salt concentration. Neither is it necessary to use de-ionized or distilled water, provided that the local tap water does not contain excessive concentrations of metals or some organic matter that imparts a strong brown color to the liquid.

Drying Cibachrome Prints

After a print has been given the important final wash treatment, it must be dried in a manner that will safeguard a flawless surface finish and physical integrity. The simplest method involves attaching a clip to the very end of one corner and letting it "drip-dry" at normal room temperature suspended from the clip. The time of drying, of course, will depend on the air temperature and relative humidity as well as on air movement, if any, but normally a print will dry in about one hour under such open-air conditions.

Drying can be speeded up through the use of a fan or even more so with a blower-type hair dryer, especially if the airstream is directed to impinge at a right angle to the print surface. This will help in removing stagnant, moist air from the print surface, thereby accelerating the diffusion of the absorbed water out of the emulsion layers. Be sure, however, that the air being blown onto the print surface is reasonably free of dust and dirt particles, which have a great tendency to adhere and become imbedded in the surface layer. With an efficient hair dryer, it is possible to dry an 8 × 10-inch Cibachrome print in about five to six minutes, but caution must be exercised, especially with Pearl-surface prints, not to heat the print to more than about 150°F; otherwise, the support and/or the gelatin structure can be degraded.

In order to avoid watermarks, some workers like to remove all surface water before drying with a squeegee, sponge, or some other smooth and soft medium. When using this procedure with Cibachrome prints, keep in mind that the wet emulsion is very delicate and that scratches or other physical damage are easily inflicted. This technique is not recommended for that reason.

Drying a Cibachrome print on a flat, horizontal surface can be done satisfactorily, provided that all the excess water has been drained from the emulsion surface before the print is laid down. Otherwise, small water droplets are apt to form in time, and these droplets can cause objectionable watermarks to show on the dry print surface due to the differential drying rates. Usually, such watermarks can be removed by soaking the print in plain water for a short while, followed by a proper drying technique.

The mirror-like finish of glossy Cibachrome-A print material is obtained without any

Figure 33. A good standard slide should include good flesh tones, neutral grays, a range of other colors, normal overall density, good sharpness, and a wide density range with detail in highlights, middle tones and shadows.

Figure 35. Your first Cibachrome print, a quadrant test, should look something like this print. Note that the quadrant test was made by exposing each section with a different lens opening: the first four lens openings on your particular enlarger lens. In this test, a 10-second exposure was used.

Also note that the color balance is incorrect and that a standard "correction" will have to be determined as explained in Chapter 7. In this case, the filter pack was taken from the Cibachrome package and was Y40 M00 C20, as indicated for Kodachrome film. To correct the color balance, Y20 was subtracted, C20 was subtracted, and M00 was left unchanged; thus, the correction for the enlarger was −Y20 and −C20.

In determining exposure, it was felt that the f/5.6 quadrant was satisfactory, and the final exposure was f/5.6 at 10 seconds.

Figure 36. The "ring-around" print guide reproduced here is a valuable guide in assisting to evaluate the density and color balance of a finished Cibachrome print.

After the print has been properly dried (a wet Cibachrome print will look more magenta-red than a completely dry one), make a comparison of your color slide and the print under the same light conditions. Hold the slide in front of a piece of white cardboard placed next to the print, and compare the slide by the light reflected from the white surface. Using this technique, you should be able to make correct conclusions about the density and the color balance of the print.

As outlined in Chapter 7, by viewing a print through various combinations of color filters you will be able to estimate what kind of color change in the filter pack will provide correct color balance. In viewing through filters, for example, if a properly exposed print is too blue, then hold a yellow filter close to your eye. The color correction should make the print look more normal. If a 20 yellow filter gives you the color balance desired, add a 20 yellow (Y20) to the filter pack. See the table on page 71 for filter changes necessary for basic color balance corrections.

+.30 too yellow

+.30 too magenta

+.30 too cyan

stop overexposed

+.30 too blue

rrect print

+.30 too green

top underexposed

+.30 too red

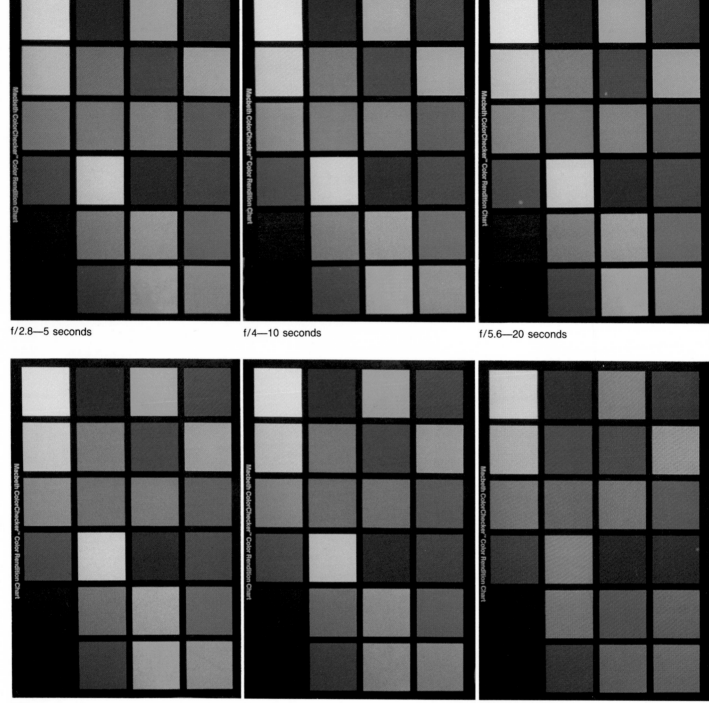

f/2.8—5 seconds

f/4—10 seconds

f/5.6—20 seconds

f/8—40 seconds

f/11—80 seconds

f/16—160 seconds

Figure 37. This series of prints illustrates the effects of reciprocity law failure with Cibachrome-A print material. The print exposure was the same for all prints, but the f-stop was changed from f/4 to f/16 in one-stop increments. The equivalent increase in exposure time from 7.5 to 120 seconds did not fully compensate for the decrease in light intensity because of reciprocity failure. The print color balance also shifted from neutral at the short exposure time to bluish-cyan at the long exposure time. To correct for the loss in effective speed and the change in color balance, print 5 was reprinted with $2\times$ the calculated exposure time and a $+10Y$ $-10C$ filter correction. The corrected print 6 matches print 1 in overall density and color balance.

Figure 42. A typical proof sheet, from which you can learn a great deal about the density and color balance of the 20 different slides on a single 8 × 10 sheet of Cibachrome print material.

slide 1: density and color satisfactory

slide 2: density and color satisfactory

slide 3: density and color satisfactory

slide 4: an Ektachrome slide which is a little too blue and slightly underexposed. Subtract Y10 and add 20% more exposure

slide 5: faces overexposed. Dodge during exposure to bring out color.

slide 6: density and color satisfactory

slide 7: density and color satisfactory

slide 8: density and color satisfactory

slide 9: two dark areas of the shell are underexposed. Burn-in these sections after initial overall exposure.

slide 10: density and color satisfactory

slide 11: density and color satisfactory

slide 12: areas at top and bottom of slide are overexposed. Dodge, or hold back light, approximately 50% of overall exposure to bring out more color.

slide 13: density and color satisfactory

slide 14: density and color satisfactory

slide 15: density and color satisfactory

slide 16: density and color satisfactory

slide 17: density and color satisfactory

slide 18: density and color satisfactory

slide 19: density and color satisfactory

slide 20: considerably underexposed. Increase exposure by at least 100%.

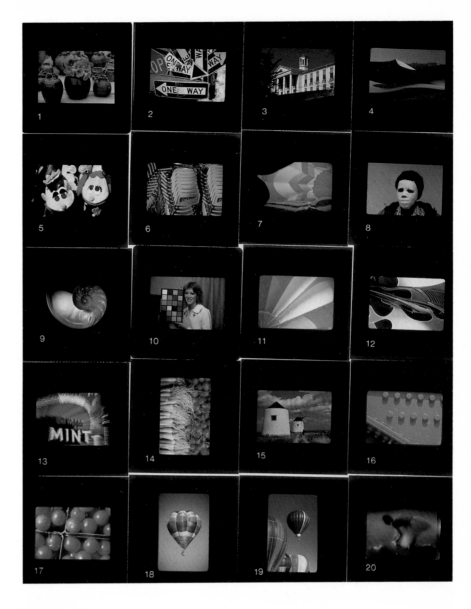

Figure 43. A straight print of a slide having a brightly lit left side, dark shadows with detail in the center section, and a neutral tone on the right side. The print was exposed for the bright and neutral tones, which left the important center area greatly underexposed. The only solution to making a satisfactory print is to burn-in the center section as shown in Figure 44. Exposure time: 30 seconds at f/5.6.

Figure 44. The same time of 30 seconds at f/5.6 was used to make the initial exposure, but the center section was burned-in for an additional 120 seconds (400%) in order to obtain detail and color.

Figure 45. A print made from a masked transparency; note the distracting image in the lower left-hand corner.

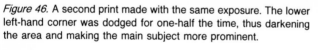

Figure 46. A second print made with the same exposure. The lower left-hand corner was dodged for one-half the time, thus darkening the area and making the main subject more prominent.

Figure 50. A photographic mask can be a very effective tool for reducing excessive highlight contrast in Cibachrome prints made from slides having a very wide density range. In this pair, the print above was made without exposure manipulation to provide reasonably good detail in middle tones and shadows. However, much highlight detail was lost. Dodging would have been difficult, because the important highlight detail in the eye region is small and spread out. The simplest and best remedy was a contrast reducing mask. The print below was made with such a mask. The print exposure of the top print was $2\times$ that of the bottom print because the mask had a maximum density of 0.3 in the highlight area.

Figure 51. Accurate reproduction of the colors of a transparency often does not give the print having the greatest impact or appeal. For example, the right-hand print of this pair certainly is much more dramatic and interesting than the left-hand print, which matches the original Kodachrome slide. To achieve the dramatic lighting in the right-hand print, a CC 50 magenta filter was used throughout the print exposure for dodging all of the sky and part of the water areas.

Figure 52. A straight print, but the sky seems to be too light.

Figure 53. The same exposure as in Figure 52, but a Cyan 50 filter was used to dodge the sky during the entire printing time.

Figure 55. Print exposure through the back of the print material. Note the overall reddish color, as only the red sensitive (cyan dye) layer of the material is affected. Also note the side reversal of the image.

Figure 56. Streaks caused by water droplets on the emulsion before the development step.

Figure 54. The title for this series of Cibachrome prints made from a Kodachrome slide could be "Variations on a Theme." The print on the left is a straight print; the sky is rather light and out of harmony with the subdued tones of the foreground. Dodging of the sky area by hand during 50 percent of the total print exposure resulted in the improved center print. In the print on the right a CC 30 cyan filter was used to dodge the sky area throughout the exposure, bringing the hue of the sky and its density into closer harmony with the foreground.

Figure 57. Print placed in processing drum incorrectly. The emulsion was placed toward the inner wall of the drum and therefore the chemistry was not evenly distributed over the print surface. In placing a Cibachrome print in a drum, the emulsion should face the inside.

Figure 58. Excessive dilution of bleach. Diluted 1:1.

Figure 59. Contamination of developer by a few drops of fixer.

Figure 60. Fixing before bleaching.

Figure 61. Print material light-struck before or during exposure.

Figure 62. A sandwich of an overexposed seascape with a slide of a cutaway chambered nautilus. Approximately twice the exposure for a normally exposed transparency is required for a sandwich of two slides.

Figure 63. A sandwich print from a black-and-white litho film positive with a slide of water rushing over pebbles in a mountain stream.

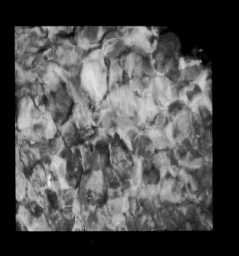

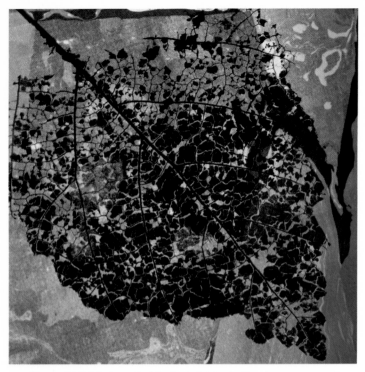

Figure 64. Print of a rotted leaf sandwiched with a transparency of a section of colored fabric. The exposure on this Cibachrome print was calculated on the transparency alone, as no compensation had to be made for the leaf.

Figure 70. Details of postage stamps or similar types of printed matter can make fascinating Cibachrome prints. In this illustration, only a section of a total stamp was used to make an unusual print that gives the appearance of a fine colored steel engraving.

Figure 66. A photogram of fall leaves, made simply by placing the leaves on a sheet of Cibachrome print material and exposing as explained in Chapter 10.

Figure 67. The same arrangement of fall leaves as in Figure 66, but textured glass was placed over the leaves to give a textured background. Normally, the use of textured glass will not increase the exposure.

Figure 72. Overprinting on Cibachrome print material is a very simple procedure, as outlined on pages 126–128, but it can be very effective in making presentations, posters, greeting and Christmas cards, and a host of other variations. In this print, black has been printed over a light area by using a "frosted" overlay sheet, and a red signature has been placed in a darker area by making a negative overlay backed by red cellophane.

Figure 68. This Cibachrome print is not a true photogram, as the background was a projected slide to give added color to the image. In projecting a transparency, it is important to select a slide or a sandwich of slides that will have similar density to the subject of the photogram. In this instance two slides had to be sandwiched so that the background would not burn out during the exposure to obtain color in the fall leaves.

Figure 69. A photomacrogram of a blue jay's feather, magnified approximately 15 times. The feather was simply mounted between glass and was projected directly onto Cibachrome print material.

Figure 71. Texture screens can be used to good advantage to change the character of a Cibachrome print, as demonstrated in this series. The print of an Italian street scene on the left is a straight print made from a 35mm Kodachrome slide. The print exposure was 15 seconds at f/9. The center print was exposed through a sheet of textured glass placed directly onto the printing material. The print exposure was 20 seconds at f/9. In the print on the right a 35mm sepia-toned Kaiser texture screen was combined with the transparency in the slide holder. Therefore, the screen pattern is enlarged by about 8×, the same as the slide image. The print exposure was 30 seconds at f/9.

Figure 75. A truly sharp and detailed Cibachrome print, made by Dr. Warren Gilson in a homemade camera. The print was made "in-camera"; that is, no transparency was used and the Cibachrome print material was exposed directly in a film holder in the camera. Dr. Gilson's procedure is outlined on pages 128–130.

Figure 76. Another example of "in-camera" use of Cibachrome print material. In this picture, titled *Susan and Ann with Matisse Towel,* Ms. Willie Anne Wright used a pinhole camera with an exposure of 3 minutes in full sun. Ms. Wright's technique is further described on page 130.

Direct Cibachrome by Dr. Warren E. Gilson.

Cibachrome pinhole photography by Willie Anne Wright.

Figure 77. Painting with light. *Crystal Construction # 1,* a lumiagraph by Mr. George Stadnik in which no camera or enlarger was used. Mr. Stadnik uses a variety of light sources, masks, and color filters to create unique and unusual images directly on Cibachrome print material.

Lumiagraph by George Stadnik.

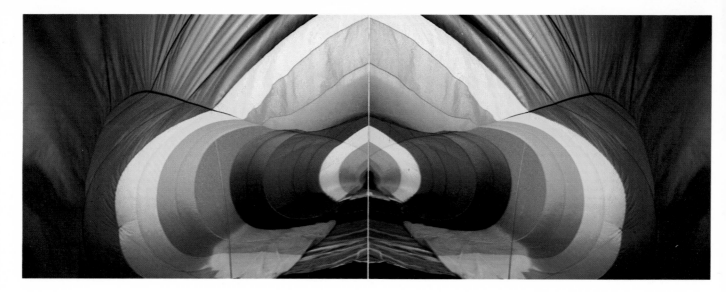

Figure 80. This "mirror" print assembly consists of two prints made from the same transparency and mounted side by side to form a continuous image. One of the prints is produced in the normal fashion, with the transparency placed emulsion side down in the slide carrier of the enlarger. The transparency position is reversed, emulsion up, for the second print. The small displacement of the film image has no noticeable effect on the print sharpness if the lens is stopped down to f/8 or more. The image size also does not change sufficiently to interfere with registration of the two print images along the common edge. It is useful, however, to allow some overlap along the common border to facilitate exact matching of detail.

Figure 81. This print quadrant consists of four prints made from the same transparency. Two of them were made with the transparency in the normal emulsion-down position in the slide carrier; the other two prints were made with the transparency in the emulsion-up position. In assembling the four prints, two matching prints are normally mounted along one diagonal of the composite image and the other two prints along the other diagonal. This gives the most satisfying structural harmony. Of course, the four prints should have the same density and color balance for best effect.

special drying procedures; it is an inherent feature of the product. Similarly, a Pearl-surface print acquires its beautiful luster without any special treatment before, during, or after drying.

Most ordinary print dryers are made for drying fiber-base black-and-white papers and are not satisfactory for Cibachrome-A prints, which have an acetate or RC paper base. Only dryers using moderately hot air that is blown onto both print surfaces, and with which the emulsion surface does not come in contact with any material, are acceptable. A hand-held hair dryer is such a device in its simplest form, but you must be careful to keep it at a safe distance from the print to prevent overheating.

Cibachrome-A Hi-Gloss prints will be quite flat after drying, but the Pearl-surface prints tend to have some face-curl. This slight curl, however, presents no problems in mounting the print.

Alternate Processing Techniques

It is to be expected that many hobbyists will develop special techniques best suited to their individual work habits and that some will also try to deviate from the standard Cibachrome P-12 chemicals for one reason or another. In fact, articles are published periodically that proclaim the advantages of one or another substitute procedure or formula. Most of the time, formula changes involve the Cibachrome P-12 developer, the main aim being a lowering of image contrast. Occasionally, other fixer formulae are suggested as a means of lowering solution costs, but bleach substitutions are not attempted because of the proprietary nature of the critical bleach catalyst.

The following comments about two suggested substitute developers are intended to provide some guidance to those interested in experimentation:

1. The first of these two black-and-white developers is Kodak Selectol-Soft at a suggested dilution of one part developer to three parts of water. A developing time of five minutes at 78°F has been recommended. This treatment does yield significantly lower image contrast than the standard Cibachrome P-12 developer at recommended dilution, time, and temperature. The minimum density of print images developed in the dilute Selectol-Soft, however, is quite high with a consequent loss of clean whites and brilliance of colors. In addition, the overall color balance tends to shift toward cyan, and highlights maintain a cold tint even after color corrections have been made to restore neutrality in medium gray tones.

2. Another conventional black-and-white developer that has been recommended is Kodak Dektol, diluted one part Dektol to one part water. Processing procedure is the same as with the Cibachrome process: at 75°F, two minutes of development, four minutes with *Cibachrome P-12* bleach, and three minutes with *Cibachrome P-12* fixer. This processing technique with Dektol 1:1 developer provides only a minimum reduction in contrast but yields a definite yellow-greenish overall cast to the print.

A similar reduction in image contrast can be obtained by increasing the dilution of the standard Cibachrome P-12 developer combined with a decrease in developing time. By the same token, image contrast can be increased (for flat transparencies) beyond normal through use of a more concentrated P-12 developer solution. These variations are summarized below:

	LOW CONTRAST	NORMAL	HIGH CONTRAST
P-12 developer, part 1A	10 ml	15 ml	20 ml
P-12 developer, part 1B	10 ml	15 ml	20 ml
Water	70 ml	60 ml	50 ml
Total volume	90 ml	90 ml	90 ml
Developing time at 75°F	1 1/2 min.	2 min.	2 1/2 min.

You should remember, however, that you will not be able to correct a really serious contrast problem by modification of the developer formula or developing time without some loss in other important image qualities. A much better, and the preferred, method of contrast control is described in detail in the next chapter.

As far as the substitution of fixer is concerned, a much more cautious approach is recommended because the consequences of such a change usually are not immediately apparent. Use of the wrong type fixer can lead to serious degradation of the image dyes in a relatively short period of time. For this reason it does not seem prudent to experiment with the fixer formula of the Cibachrome P-12 process. Satisfy your impulse for experimentation in safer and more rewarding phases of printing and processing!

CHAPTER 9

More About Exposure and Processing

There are a number of special exposure techniques that can be valuable or even necessary for obtaining the best possible quality from many slides. These techniques are described in the following paragraphs so that you may be aware of their applicability to Cibachrome printing, their potential benefits, and their limitations.

THE PROOF SHEET

Proof-printing is considered an essential preliminary step in working with black-and-white or color negatives because it provides information about many quality aspects of the negative images that is not readily apparent from an inspection of the negatives themselves. With positive color transparencies, however, the image can be evaluated directly, so the great value of proof-printing is not recognized by many workers for this reason. A proof sheet made on Cibachrome-A material from a whole group of slides can give you a wealth of information that will be of great assistance in the subsequent preparation of enlargements. You can proof-print 20 mounted or 36 unmounted 35mm frames on a single sheet of 8×10-inch Cibachrome-A material and from it be able to derive the following data for each slide: the proper exposure for enlarged prints, the best filter balance, and necessary modifications in density or contrast in parts or all of the image.

By following the procedure outlined below you will also be able, in many instances, to proceed directly from the proof sheet to the final enlargement. In all other cases you will have a good indication of the specific changes in exposure and/or color balance required to obtain the desired results in the final print. Clearly, the beginner as well as the professional will save time, effort, and costs by adopting proof-printing as a standard routine in Cibachrome print-making.

Procedure for Making a Proof Sheet

1. If you plan to use mounted slides, we recommend that you employ the homemade

easel as described previously together with a sheet of thin glass such as a window pane. If you plan to proof 36 frames in strip form, you may use the same equipment or one of the numerous proof-printers available through photo shops. With the latter you simply insert the film strips into the proof-printer and proceed with the normal exposure sequence.

2. Next you should adjust and focus your enlarger as if you were making an 8 × 10-inch print from a full-frame 35mm transparency.

3. Select the proper filter pack for the type of transparencies you intend to proof-print (for example, Kodachrome or Ektachrome) and the particular batch of Cibachrome print material that you will use later on for the final enlargements.

4. Adjust the lens stop and exposure time for the exposure you have found correct for an 8 × 10-inch print from a normal slide.

5. If you are using a homemade easel and a sheet of 8 × 10-inch glass, place the 20 mounted slides on the glass *in room light;* it is almost impossible to align them properly in darkness. Keep the glass with slides on top of it near the printing easel (see Figures 40 and 41).

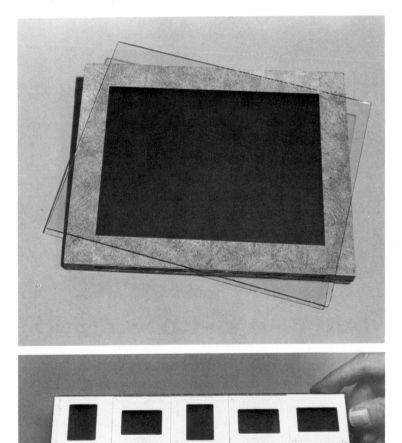

Figure 40. A useful accessory for use with the homemade border-less easel described in Chapter 6 is a piece of clear glass cut to exactly the same size as the easel. For example, if an 8 × 10-inch easel is made, have a glass cutter cut an 8 × 10 piece of glass (and ask him to sand the edges to avoid finger cuts). This piece of glass is especially helpful in proofing slides.

Figure 41. To make a contact proof-sheet of twenty mounted slides, first place them on a sheet of 8 × 10-inch glass in room light; when printing, carefully position the glass on the easel over the sheet of Cibachrome print material.

6. In total darkness remove an 8 × 10-inch sheet of Cibachrome-A material from its package, place it on the easel, and then carefully position the glass holding the slides on top of the Cibachrome sheet.

7. Expose the Cibachrome material, set the glass and slides aside, insert the Cibachrome sheet into the processing drum, and process as usual.

The print made in this fashion will be a contact proof of 20 slides. Even though the transparencies will not have been in intimate contact with the print material, good sharpness will be obtained because the exposing light is nearly parallel when the enlarger lamphouse is at the height required for an 8 × magnification. When the proof print is dry, evaluate each small print image critically, making notes about any necessary changes in exposure and filtration and any local or overall density or contrast modifications. If there are no corrections needed, which will happen quite frequently, a full 8 × 10-inch enlargement can be made with exactly the same settings used for proof-printing—that is, the same magnification, the same exposure, and the same filtration will produce an 8 × 10-inch enlargement having the same overall density and color balance as the small proof print!

Those slides that did not yield entirely satisfactory proof prints can be printed with good knowledge of the required corrections, including local dodging or burning-in or overall contrast masking. Figure 42 on page 95 shows a section of a typical proof sheet with appropriate annotations for each slide.

Another useful byproduct of a proof sheet is the small prints themselves; these are well suited for making attractive pieces of jewelry, such as stickpins, tie tacks, cufflinks, and earrings, to mention a few of the possible applications.

MANIPULATION DURING PRINTING

Very few fine photographic prints, be they black-and-white or color, are straight prints; most require some local and/or overall correction before, during, or after exposure. This is fortunate in a way because it represents a challenge to your creative abilities and, therefore, provides great satisfaction in the end.

Correction can be accomplished in many ways—by dodging, burning-in, masking, flashing, and others. Most of these corrective measures are used to modify overall or local tone or color reproduction. Each technique will be discussed separately to provide a clear understanding of its capabilities as well as its limitations.

Dodging

Those who have experience with dodging from black-and-white or color negative printing must reverse their thinking when it comes to dodging a Cibachrome print. This is so because the term dodging refers to the darkening of a portion of a photographic print image through a selective change in print exposure. Special dodging tools are normally used for small areas and fingers or hands for large areas. In negative printing the darkening of the local area is achieved by giving more than the overall print exposure, but in the direct-positive Cibachrome system darkening, or dodging, is accomplished by reducing the print exposure in the local areas.

Burning-in

Burning-in, on the other hand, refers to lightening a portion of a print image. In negative printing this is secured by decreasing the print exposure in the selected portion, but in Cibachrome printing it requires the reverse procedure, that is, an increase in print exposure above that used for the entire image. Again, special devices can be bought or made for burning-in, or the hands can be used in simple cases.

More About Dodging and Burning-in

Dodging and burning-in are the simplest control techniques for local tone correction and they are useful in the majority of instances. The choice between the two will depend on the characteristics of the slide being printed. For example, if one of your slides has important highlight as well as shadow details that cannot be retained in a straight print, you will have to decide whether it is easier to dodge the highlights or burn-in the shadows (see Figure 43 on page 95). Notice that the print reproduced in this illustration has an area of highlights on the left side, dark shadows with significant detail in the center, and middle tones on the right side. It was impossible to retain detail in all of these areas in a straight print, so an exposure was used that would secure good detail rendition in the highlights and middle tones.

In the second print additional exposure was given to the shadow areas by burning-in. This procedure was adopted because it was simpler in this instance to burn-in the well-defined shadow area than to dodge the two separate highlight and middle-tone areas (see Figure 44 on page 95). With another slide it may be better to use a basic print exposure that ensures optimum reproduction of shadow detail and to dodge the highlight regions during part of the main exposure.

With experience you will learn to judge when and where dodging or burning-in can provide improved tone reproduction. Some print-makers go so far as to routinely darken the corners of all of their prints in order to enhance the relative brightness of the print centers. Many more darken or lighten selected sections of print images or even distinct image elements, such as tree trunks, the eyes or lips in portraits, the foam on breaking waves, or a cluttered background to suppress distracting image elements or accentuate areas of interest (see Figures 45 and 46 on page 96).

While dodging or burning-in, remember to keep your tool or your hands in constant slow motion to prevent the formation of noticeable density gradients or sharp lines of demarcation. Fortunately, owing to its soft gradation, Cibachrome-A print material is very tolerant of exposure variations, and with a little care you will be able to prevent detection of your exposure manipulations. You will be aided by the good contrast balance of Cibachrome-A print material and its modest reciprocity failure, which will assure that the same color balance is maintained in the differently exposed areas.

In summary, dodging and burning-in are simple and often very useful techniques for improving the tone reproduction in your Cibachrome prints, and you should make every effort to master them. Remember that a contact proof sheet can be a very helpful guide in choosing the best procedure before you make the first large print.

Masking

Some color slide images, however, present tone reproduction problems that cannot be corrected either by dodging or burning-in, notably when small and intricate detail must be retained in a number of highlight and/or shadow areas. The only really satisfactory and effective remedy in such instances is a contrast mask. Unfortunately, many hobbyists shy away from masking, believing that it involves a difficult and complicated procedure. In reality, it is a simple and valuable technique that can be readily applied by anyone who is engaged in color printing.

In Cibachrome printing the normal mask is a low-contrast black-and-white negative that encompasses only the highlight and light middle-tone portions of the color slide image. Its purpose and function can be visualized from the schematic diagram (Figure 47).

The original gray-scale "A," shown on the top, has ten steps of 0.3 density increment: step 1 has a density of 0.0 and step 11 a density of 3.0. (In an actual color transparency image these values would be closer to 0.2 and 3.2, but the other values are being used here for ease of explanation.)

The mask "B", as shown in the center, is a negative of "A" in which only the low density steps 1 through 5 are recorded. The contrast of the mask image is kept at a low level by developing the exposed black-and-white film for a relatively short

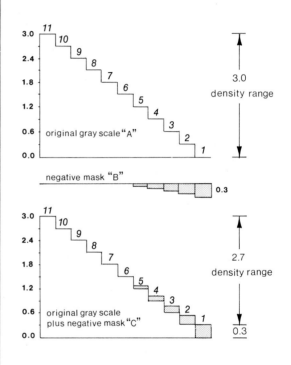

Figure 47.

113

time in a diluted developer solution. These conditions are adjusted to yield a maximum mask density of 0.3 in step 1.

When the original "A" and the mask "B" are combined, as in "C", the contrast of the steps in region 1 to 5 is reduced by about 25 percent, and the density range of the entire scale "A" is reduced by about 10 percent.

When a Cibachrome print is made from a high-contrast but properly masked transparency, it will exhibit good detail in all portions of the tone scale. If the mask image has a maximum density of 0.3, the print exposure will be twice that needed for a print made without the mask. This will be so because the additional density of 0.3 in the highlights will reduce the intensity of the printing light by a factor of 2, and the print must be exposed sufficiently to have good whites. Of course, the maximum mask density will vary somewhat if a fixed exposure and developing procedure is used with all slides, depending on the highlight densities of the slides. These variations tend to be small, however, and a fixed masking procedure is practical and recommended for that reason.

In summary, a low-contrast negative silver mask can be a very good means for improving the tone reproduction in Cibachrome prints made from high-contrast transparencies. A maximum, fixed-mask density of about 0.3 is useful for this purpose and convenient because it entails a simple doubling of the normal print exposure.

Equipment and Materials Required for Masking

Contrast reducing masks for Cibachrome printing are best prepared by contact printing. Registration of the finished mask and the original color transparency will be facilitated if the mask image is made *unsharp.* Moreover, an unsharp mask actually enhances apparent sharpness in the final print image because the contrast of edges and of small detail is not decreased by the mask; only the large-area contrast is reduced.

The following materials are needed for mask preparation:
- A contact printing frame, preferably of 4×5-inch size
- Frosted acetate film sheeting or some other translucent, white material
- Black-and-white, panchromatic sheet film (4×5-inch size), such as Ilford FP-4, Kodak Plus-X, or Kodak Pan-Masking film
- Black-and-white film developer, such as Ilford ID-11 Plus or Kodak D-76
- Film fixer, such as Ilford or Kodak acid hardening fixing-bath
- Three film processing trays (4×5-inch size) or a sheet-film processing tank and sheet-film holders

These items are optional:
- Kodak 1.0 neutral density filter (3×3 inches)
- Kodak calibrated film gray-scale

Procedure for Preparation of a Contrast-Reducing Mask

1. Select a 35mm slide from which you have already made a Cibachrome print having satisfactory overall density and color balance but excessive image contrast.

2. Place the slide into your enlarger and focus it sharply on top of the print that you have positioned on the easel.

3. Put the same filter pack into the enlarger that yielded the satisfactory color balance of the first print (assuming that you still have unexposed material of the same batch number; otherwise adjust the filter pack appropriately).

4. If you have a 1.0 neutral density filter, add it to the filter pack. If you have a color head enlarger, set the filter dials to the appropriate marks and place the 1.0 neutral density filter next to the enlarger for later use or mount it temporarily under the lens.

5. Remove the slide from the enlarger and take it out of its mount.

6. Tape the transparency(ies) *emulsion-side up* onto a 4×5-inch piece of frosted acetate or equivalent material (you can fasten up to six 35mm frames onto one 4×5-inch sheet).

7. Place the acetate sheet carrying the transparencies into the contact printing frame with the emulsion of the transparency facing the cover glass of the printing frame.

8. If you are using a 1.0 neutral density filter, stop your lens down by one full f-stop compared with the stop used for the original Cibachrome print. For example, if you had used f/5.6, stop down to f/8. This is necessary because the total exposure of the mask film should be only 1/20th of the proper Cibachrome print exposure.

If you do not have a 1.0 neutral density filter, adjust your lens aperture and exposure time to any combination that will provide 1/20th of the original print exposure. For instance, if you change the f-stop from f/5.6 to f/11 (a factor of 4 in terms of light intensity), you will have to decrease the exposure time by a factor of 5 (4×5=20).

A change of three full f-stops, such as f/16 from f/5.6, will require an exposure time reduction of 2.5 times (8×2.5=20). Thus, if the original Cibachrome exposure was 20 seconds at f/5.6, you would use 20 seconds at f/8 with the 1.0 neutral density filter or 4 seconds at f/11 or 8 seconds at f/16 without the filter.

9. Position the contact printing frame containing the acetate slide assembly at the center of the enlarger easel with the spring-fastened back cover nearby.

10. Set the timer for the required mask film exposure as explained above.

11. Turn out the lights, and place a sheet of unexposed black-and-white film *emulsion-side up* onto the back side of the frosted acetate sheet.

12. Place a sheet of black paper over the black-and-white film sheet (the black interleafing paper in the sheet film box will suffice).

13. Close the contact printing frame with the spring-actuated back.

14. Turn over the printing frame and expose. The various elements should be arranged as shown below:

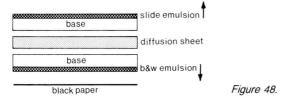

Figure 48.

15. After exposure, remove the black-and-white film and process it in a tray or tank according to the following recommendation:

- Develop for two minutes at 68°F in Ilford ID-11 Plus or Kodak D-76 diluted 1:2 with constant agitation
- Immerse for 30 seconds in an acetic acid short-stop bath or in plain water at 68°F
- Fix in an acid hardening film fixing-bath for twice the clearing time (about five minutes at 68°F with agitation)
- Wash in running water for 10 minutes at 65° to 70°F
- Dry in a dust-free atmosphere

16. The maximum density of the mask image should be near 0.30. You can measure film densities with a transmission densitometer, or you can estimate them by visually comparing the darkest area on the mask image with the steps of a calibrated gray-scale or with a 0.30 Kodak neutral density filter. A reasonable estimate can also be made by comparing the film density with a filter pack consisting of Y30, M30, and C30 color correction filters. Such a filter pack will tend to have a reddish cast, however, and is not as useful as a neutral density scale or neutral filter.

Printing With a Masked Transparency

The printing of a masked color transparency is quite straightforward. The mask is first registered with the transparency on a light table, and the two are taped together back-to-back along one side of the assembly. Registration is particularly simple with 35mm frames by matching the outlines of the sprocket holes. Moreover, the unsharpness of the mask image makes registration easier and less critical. The transparency-plus-mask is then mounted in a glass-type 35mm slide binder, such as the Gepe, and is placed into the slide carrier of the enlarger with the transparency on the bottom (see diagram below).

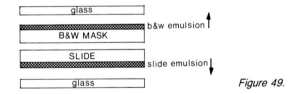

Figure 49.

The first print from the masked transparency should be given twice the exposure used for the original non-masked print. The filter balance may have to be adjusted to offset any selective absorption of the silver image of the mask. Often a yellow filter will have to be added, but this can vary from one worker to another. In any event, some experience with printing masked transparencies will provide pertinent information about average exposure and color-balance adjustments required with a specific set of conditions. Figure 50 on page 96 illustrates the use of a mask to reduce excessive highlight contrast.

Flashing

Flashing is a technique used in color printing for any of the following purposes: to correct a lack of color contrast balance in a slide or print material, to lighten the shadow areas of a print, or to obtain duocolor or monochrome effects.

No matter what the purpose, the basic procedure for flashing is the same in all instances and involves exposing the entire print uniformly to diffuse blue, green, or red light or a mixture of such light. The intensity of the blue, green, or red light is adjusted, or the exposure time is varied in accordance with the intended purpose and may range from 1/100th of a normal print exposure to more than that exposure when extreme effects are wanted. For example, if only a small correction in the color balance of shadow areas is wanted, a weak or short flash is used, but if a monochromatic image is desired, enough flash exposure will be required to burn out two of the three dye layers. Thus, enough blue and red light flashing would have to be used to completely expose all silver halides in the blue- and red-sensitive emulsions of Cibachrome material if only a magenta dye image is to remain in the final print.

So-called sharp-cutting color filters are used in flashing in order to limit the action of the flashing exposure to the proper image layers. The following Kodak filters are useful for the indicated purpose:

> Kodak Wratten filter 47 or 47B (blue) to reduce yellow density
> Kodak Wratten filter 58 (green) to reduce magenta density
> Kodak Wratten filter 25 or 29 (red) to reduce cyan density
> Kodak Wratten filter 16 (yellow) to reduce blue density
> Kodak Wratten filter 33 (magenta) to reduce green density
> Color compensating filter 100C (cyan) to reduce red density

The flash exposure, as mentioned, must be uniformly apportioned over the entire print. It can be given before or after the main print exposure. The following procedure is recommended:

1. Make a normal exposure from the slide that requires corrective print flashing.
2. Place the exposed print into a light-tight container, such as your processing drum.
3. Remove the slide from the slide carrier of your enlarger.
4. Place the proper sharp-cutting filter into the filter holder or under the enlarger lens and adjust the f-stop and exposure timer.
5. Turn out the room lights and reposition the Cibachrome print on the enlarger easel.
6. Make the flash exposure.
7. Process the print normally.

Two quality deficiencies of color transparencies are most amenable to correction by print flashing: colored shadows resulting from peculiar lighting conditions at the time of camera exposure and imbalance of color contrast caused by poor storage of the film before exposure, deficient processing, or long or improper storage after processing. For example, a slide image may have very blue shadows because the shaded portion of the original scene was illuminated only by deep blue sky light. This color cast will be much more noticeable and objectionable in a reflection color print than in the projected screen image of the slide because of the differences in viewing conditions. You can improve such a print by flashing it with yellow light, that is, with a Kodak Wratten yellow filter No. 16. Of course, the optimum amount of flash exposure will depend upon the extent of required correction, which is not easily estimated by visual assessment of the image. Therefore, a test print is normally required, and it is advisable to try several different flash exposures rather than to guess at just one value. A sensible procedure consists of dividing the print image into six horizontal or vertical sections, five of which are given increasing amounts of flash exposure while the sixth is given only the main exposure for reference purposes. The smallest flash exposure should be about 1/100th of the main print exposure, and each of the other four sections should receive about twice the exposure of its neighbor, providing the following flash exposure series: 1/100; 1/50; 1/25; 1/10; 1/5 of the main print exposure.

The question is asked at times as to whether flashing can be used to reduce the overall contrast of a Cibachrome print. It is possible to reduce shadow contrast by this means and thereby the apparent overall contrast, but this is not a good remedy because print quality normally will suffer more than it will gain from such remedial treatment. The proper method for reducing excessive print contrast is masking, which does not reduce the density range of the print. A reduction in print development also offers some control over excessive print-image contrast, but is more effective in highlight regions than in other parts of the tonal scale.

In summary, print flashing can be of value only in very special cases and tends to be a rather time-consuming and costly technique.

Local Correction of Color

At times you may want to modify the color of just a small section of a Cibachrome print rather than its overall color balance. For example, the sky of an otherwise excellent print of a landscape may be too light and lacking in blue shading. You can make the sky darker and at the same time give it a more saturated blue color by dodging the sky area during the main print exposure with a blue filter. The extent of correction will depend upon the density of the filter and the fraction of the time used for dodging. When applying this technique, be sure to keep the filter in motion during dodging so as to avoid a sharp line of demarcation between the dodged and undodged areas. Of course, if you don't have a blue filter, you can use a combination of magenta and cyan printing filters, and you can choose a filter density that best fits the job at hand (see Figures 51–54 on pages 97–99). Similarly, the color saturation of a yellow flower or even a petal of a flower can be increased by dodging with a yellow filter during the normal print exposure.

If the color of a shadow area needs to be accented, a supplemental exposure (that is, burning-in) with a color filter can be utilized. For this purpose it is best to have a fairly large piece of cardboard or the like with an aperture near the center over which the filter can be taped. The opaque cardboard will have to be held sufficiently close to the lens to shield all but the selected shadow area from the printing light. This kind of dodging can be considered localized print flashing, and in extreme cases it may be necessary to use sharp-cutting filters rather than color compensating filters. And just as in flashing, you may find it necessary to make a test print or two in order to find the best exposure combination.

CONTACT PRINTING

If you have positive color transparencies in sizes from 4×5- to 8×10-inches, you can make outstanding Cibachrome prints from them by contact printing. For this purpose a conventional contact printing frame is very useful, but an ordinary glass pane can also be employed for keeping the transparency and print material in intimate contact during print exposure. Of course, the glass must be clean and free of striations, which would be imaged in the print. Since Cibachrome-A print material lies quite flat, especially the Hi-Gloss type, it is easy to ensure good overall contact between the film and printing material without too much pressure.

If you use your enlarger as a light source for contact printing, as discussed in the chapter dealing with proof-printing, the f-stop, exposure time, and filter balance will be the same as you would use in making an enlargement from the same transparency. Just remember that the total exposure will have to be about 7.5 foot-candle-seconds and that the filter balance will be governed by the color balance of the Cibachrome material and the brand of color film. It will be necessary, of course, to raise the enlarger head high enough to provide even illumination over the entire image area. With condenser-type enlargers this can be achieved more easily by defocusing the lens so that the lamp will not be imaged sharply on the easel.

COMMON PROBLEMS IN PRINT-MAKING AND THEIR CORRECTION

There is no question that the exposing and processing of Cibachrome-A material is really quite simple; nevertheless, problems are bound to arise from time to time, and beginners especially are apt to make mistakes. The mistakes that are made tend to occur in definite patterns and at certain frequencies; therefore, it is possible to provide a list that includes the majority of problems one is likely to encounter. This list and illustrations of the mistakes are presented on pages 98–100. The causes of the mistakes and remedial actions are given to help identification and correction.

Other less common mistakes include improper mixing of chemical solutions, use of old or exhausted solutions, and use of defective printing or processing equipment. Of these, the inadvertent use of improperly mixed solutions can be the most subtle and vexing problem; for this reason a procedure for checking the quality of processing solutions is outlined below.

How to Check the Quality of Suspect Processing Solutions

If you have produced a series of Cibachrome prints that appear to suffer from the same or very similar defects, it is possible that a processing problem is the cause. Of course, the printing material itself may be defective because it is too old, has not been stored properly, or has a manufacturing defect or some other undetected malfunction. But if several prints suddenly have low contrast or a bluish color balance or bluish blacks, suspect your processing solutions. Improper storage of the packaged chemicals or mixed solutions or a mixing mistake or contamination are some of the possible causes of processing problems. Whatever the reason, it is necessary to determine which solution(s) is (are) at fault. But how does one check the quality of processing solutions without chemical test equipment? Use the simple photographic cross-checking procedure described below.

First, a word of advice: Don't throw away suspected solutions before you have ascertained which, if any, is really defective. If you follow your natural impulse and dump all solutions in favor of a fresh mix, you will likely discard some perfectly good chemicals as well as all the evidence about the cause of the problem.

Unless you have some other indication, it would be best to check the developer first. To do this, proceed as follows:

1. Prepare a small quantity of fresh developing solution from unopened bottles of developer concentrates 1A and 1B—say, enough for processing six 4×5-inch prints.

2. Make two 4×5-inch prints from your standard test slide using the same normal exposure and filter values.

3. Develop one of the two prints in a tray or drum with the freshly mixed developer and the second print in the old, possibly defective, developer.

4. Bleach, fix, and wash both prints identically and dry them as usual.

5. Mark each print on the back side with pertinent exposure and processing data.

Inspection of the finished prints will reveal whether or not the old developer is the source of your problem. If it produced the same defect noticed before while the freshly prepared developer produced satisfactory results, it will be reasonable to conclude that the old developer *and the developer alone* was at fault. If both prints exhibit the troublesome defect, however, you will have to check the bleach and, if need be, the fixer. The same method outlined for checking the developer will be suitable, except that you will be comparing a freshly prepared bleach solution with the old one or a fresh fixer with an old fixer solution.

An experienced darkroom worker can carry out all three comparisons in one processing run by using four test prints and processing them in the following manner:

1. Fresh developer, fresh bleach, and fresh fixer
2. *Old developer,* fresh bleach, and fresh fixer
3. Fresh developer, *old bleach,* and fresh fixer
4. Fresh developer, fresh bleach, and *old fixer*

Of course, this procedure requires more processing trays or drums and a good print identification system (such as cut corners), but it does provide all the answers in one sitting. Once you have identified the defective solution, file the test prints for future reference or send them to the manufacturer of the chemicals for further review and comment.

CHAPTER 10

Creative and Experimental Techniques

Y ou will get a great amount of pleasure and personal satisfaction from your creative and experimental efforts in using Cibachrome, as it offers many opportunities for expressing your imagination. Since Cibachrome is a positive-to-positive printing method, you will be able to previsualize your final results in many cases.

Combining or "Sandwiching" Slides

Combining two different slides to make a single photographic image is a very good example of how you can see in advance the effect you can obtain in the final print. One of the primary advantages of "sandwiching" is the opportunity of using a relatively poor slide, especially in the case of overexposure, and combining it with another to create a new and oftentimes very interesting image.

In Figure 62 on page 101, you would probably classify the first subject of a seascape as a "throw-away" slide. It was taken on a moving boat with a hand-held 35mm camera and a 500mm mirror telephoto lens and is not exactly needle-sharp. But by combining it with a slide of a cutaway chambered nautilus, an interesting new print is created.

In Figure 63 on page 101, another technique is used, combining a black-and-white litho film positive with a slide of water rushing over pebbles in a mountain stream. The concept for the final print was to convey the feeling of an old, faded black-and-white print that might have been found in the attic after many years of neglect.

In Figure 64 on page 102, in another variation of "sandwiching," an actual rotted leaf is combined with a transparency of a section of brightly colored cloth. Because of the size of the leaf itself, a 2 1/4 × 2 1/4-inch transparency had to be used in this instance.

In all of these illustrations, note that one element of the "sandwich" has low density, either because of overexposure in the case of the boat, virtually no middle tones in the case of the wagon wheels, or no density other than the leaf in Figure 64.

You will appreciate from these examples that it is a good idea to save overexposed slides and even to purposely overexpose some subjects, such as textures and patterns, which may be used later for combining with other transparencies.

Another form of "sandwiching" is to add a low-density filter or light-colored cellophane to a slide to change the overall color balance of a print.

All "sandwiched" combinations must be placed in glass slide binders, such as a Gepe binder, or between glass and bound with tape, as it is absolutely necessary to keep all the elements of the combination in close contact with one another for good overall image sharpness.

Generally, a "sandwich" combination requires approximately twice the exposure of a properly exposed single transparency, but varying, of course, with the overall densities of each of the elements. When combining the leaf and the colored swatch, the density of the swatch was the dominant exposure factor.

Photograms

Photograms in full color are another of the versatile qualities of the Cibachrome positive-to-positive system, and full-size reproductions of flowers, leaves, and any other objects that transmit light can be made quickly and easily.

Keep in mind that you will generally have no transparency in the enlarger and will be using "white" light that can pass through and around objects that you may consider very dense, such as a rhododendron leaf.

On photograms, you are using transmitted light (through the object, whereas normally you will be viewing the object itself by *reflected* light), so you cannot expect the final reproduction to be an exact match of what you see in this viewing mode. Nevertheless, the colors obtainable in a Cibachrome photogram can be brilliant and sometimes even more pleasing than the colors seen by reflected light.

As has been stated often, Cibachrome print material must be exposed in total darkness, yet one of the most important aspects to consider in making photograms is the pleasing arrangement of the subject matter, which is virtually impossible to achieve if you can't see what you are doing!

This is again an application of the homemade easel and a piece of glass that is exactly the same size as the easel.

Using the special easel and glass, the step-by-step procedure for making a photogram is as follows:

1. Arrange your subject matter on the piece of clean glass, carefully removing any dust spots, pollen (in case of flowers), etc., as any foreign matter will show as black spots. When you have satisfactorily completed your arrangement, *turn off the lights.*

2. Place a sheet of Cibachrome-A print material on the easel emulsion-side up.

3. Carefully lift the glass with the arrangement and place it on the print material and easel. With the glass, the print material, and the easel all the same size, it will be simple, even in the dark, to fit them all in place. At this point, you have the choice of leaving the arrangement, if it is flowers or leaves, dimensionally "free," or you may place another piece of glass over the subject matter to press it in closer contact with the print material.

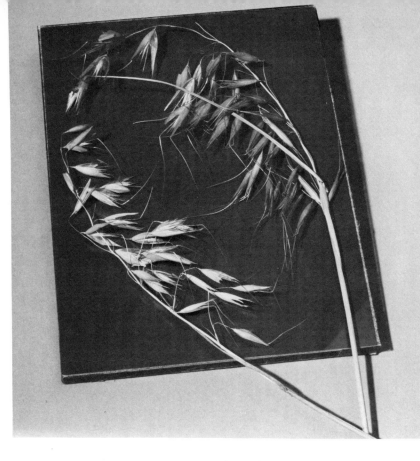

Figure 65. Another important use of the home-made borderless easel and matching size glass is in the making of photograms. As the illustration shows, it is quite easy to arrange subjects for photograms on the glass in room light, and then register the glass with the easel.

4. Make the exposure.

5. Lift off the glass and arrangement; carefully lay it aside. Try not to disturb the position of the subject matter, as you may want to make additional prints.

6. Remove the print material and place it into the processing drum.

7. When the exposed material is in the drum and the end caps are securely in place, turn on the lights and process.

When the print has been processed and dried, you will note that the background (the whole area not covered by the subject matter) will be "burned out" and therefore white (see Figure 66 on page 102). You may or may not like this effect, but you do have options of adding tone or color to the background:

1. Tone or texture may be added to the background simply by placing a piece of textured glass (such as shower-stall textured glass available at most glass dealers) over the entire arrangement and exposing the print through the glass (see Figure 67 on page 102). Different types of textured glass will give different effects and you may want to experiment. Normally, use of the textured glass will not require an increase in exposure.

2. To add brilliant color or perhaps even a background image, you can project a slide onto your photogram arrangement, rather than using uniform "white" light (see Figure 68 on page 103). The key point to remember in this "projection" technique is to select a transparency that has proper overall density, for if it is too thin, the image detail will be lost by the time sufficient exposure has been given for the main objects of the photogram. If the slide is too dense, on the other hand, there will be insufficient exposure for recording the details of the photogram arrangement. Very likely you will need to do some dodging and burning-in when you use a projected transparency image as the exposing light for a photogram.

The colors of a photogram image often differ markedly from those of the original objects viewed under normal conditions. This happens because the photogram is created by light that has passed through the objects, whereas your normal perception of objects is based on light that is reflected by them, and, as noted, the color distribution of transmitted and reflected light can be quite dissimilar. For example, many bird feathers exhibit brilliant hues when viewed by reflected light due to interference phenomena, the same kind of physical interaction between light waves that accounts for the iridescent colors of soap bubbles and oil slicks. Interference usually does not occur in the light transmitted by bird feathers, however, and therefore photograms made from them often are almost totally devoid of color differentiation. Of course, you may still obtain a very interesting print because of the intricate structure and fine detail of the image.

You are much less likely to encounter such large and startling differences between the colors obtained with reflected and transmitted light exposure when the colors result from the presence of dyes or other colorants inside the objects, as in the blossoms and leaves of most plants. The Cibachrome photograms of fall leaves, shown in Figure 66 on page 102, for example, have very nearly the coloration seen in the original objects viewed by reflected light. Of course, you may want to shift or change the colors in the photogram deliberately to accentuate certain hues or for some other unusual effect. It is advisable, however, to start with your normal filter pack as used with your standard slide and to make changes in overall or local color balance only after you have seen what the "normal" photogram exposure produces.

When you do add filters or use another technique for color control, keep in mind that a filter change will affect the entire image, so that the intensification of red colors, for instance, through the addition of a red filter will also cause a degradation of green and blue colors. Careful application of such interpretive techniques can be quite rewarding. In making photograms, you have the opportunity to apply your artistic talents in creative color as well as designs.

The exposure required for photograms varies with a number of factors:

1. The intensity of the enlarger light.

2. The distance of the lamphouse from the baseboard (be sure you have even illumination on the easel with light coverage at least two inches beyond each side).

3. The lens aperture and focus setting (it is well to "defocus" in order to improve the evenness of illumination) and, of course, the opacity of the objects. Remember that the amount of light transmitted by thin objects, such as the petals and leaves of a poinsettia, will be substantially greater than the amount transmitted by thick objects, such as the large blossoms and fleshy leaves of a rhododendron or tulip. In fact, you may have to remove some petals at times in order to obtain sufficient light transmission and, therefore, sufficient exposure in some areas of the photogram.

Keep in mind also that in working with photograms, you are dealing mostly with translucent rather than transparent objects with a consequent increase in scattering of the transmitted light. The exposure received by the Cibachrome material also will depend on whether or not you use a cover glass, because as the objects are brought closer to the surface of the Cibachrome emulsion, the light intensity will increase and the required exposure time decrease.

Taking all the foregoing factors into consideration, a good starting point for a photogram exposure is twice that for a print of equal size made from a standard-type slide. For example, if your exposure for an 8×10-inch print normally is 30 seconds at f/5.6, start with 30 seconds at f/4 for a photogram of reasonably translucent flowers; subsequently, you can make adjustments in color balance and exposure to suit your taste.

You will find that increases in exposure often will result in more color saturation in the photogram and in bringing out subtle color shadings and structural details that are lost in images having greater overall density.

As mentioned previously, you have the option of leaving your objects, particularly flowers and leaves, dimensionally "free" or placing a piece of glass over the entire arrangement in order to obtain more intimate contact between the objects and the Cibachrome print material. An "unrestrained" spray of flowers and leaves will produce a photogram having the quality of an abstract watercolor painting with few sharp lines and details. The main disadvantage will be the required increase in exposure, which can be substantial if the flowers are more than an inch above the print material. You may find it necessary to gently bend or even break a branch to bring a flower or leaf closer to the emulsion surface.

On the other hand, by placing a piece of glass (heavy plate glass, if available) over the composition, you can obtain sharper outlines and more detail in coloration and patterns. Again, to emphasize, less exposure is required when the objects are in direct contact with the print material.

In summary, photograms can be very creative and satisfying with Cibachrome-A print material, and the technique is quite simple to master. Remember that each photogram is *an original* because it is very unlikely that you will ever make two exactly the same!

Photomacrograms

Photomacrograms (perhaps a new word in photographic color printing) are prints made directly on Cibachrome without using a photographic transparency, but by projecting an image of a translucent object placed in the slide carrier directly onto the print material. There are a number of interesting options with this technique and, depending upon your enlarger and your lens, you can obtain images at up to 20 to 30 times magnification. For example, Figure 69 on page 103 shows a photomacrogram of a section of a blue jay's feather magnified approximately 15 times.

In Figure 70 on page 102, a very small portion of a postage stamp that had been mounted in a plastic slide mount is shown. Before placing it in the glass mount, the stamp was slightly impregnated with silicon to increase the translucency of the paper.

The reproduction on page 102 (see Figure 64) was made from a "sandwich" combination print of a rotted leaf and a transparency—still another variation of the photomacrogram technique.

In making photomacrograms, you must remember again that you are working with transmitted light, and you will face the same conditions as with photograms. For example, in the illustration on page 103 (see Figure 69), you will note that the blue and gray colors seen on a blue jay feather by reflected light turn to brownish hues in the print exposed with transmitted light.

The basic filter pack for photomacrograms should be your standard Kodachrome pack with the opportunity to vary it according to the desired aesthetic effect. Exposure will depend upon the subject matter. For example, the postage stamp illustration required only about one-third the exposure of a well-exposed 35mm slide.

Use of Texture Screens With Cibachrome

Texture screens are quite simple to use with Cibachrome and can give you a number of interesting effects. Although most commercially available texture screens are designed for use with negatives, they will work equally well with the Cibachrome positive-to-positive system.

There are two types of screens, and each type is available in a wide variety of textures:

1. The first type is placed in contact with the surface of the print material during exposure. These screens are rather difficult to obtain and are expensive because of their size. They are made in sizes of 8×10 inches to 20×24 inches.

2. The other type screen, readily available at most photo dealers, is "sandwiched" directly with the slide; its pattern is superimposed on the projected image of the slide. Among the brands available are Paterson and Kaiser screens, each in a number of textures, including the popular tweed, linen, tapestry, etc.

The pattern of the "sandwiched" texture screen will be enlarged, of course, and will increase as you increase the magnification of the primary slide image, whereas the pattern of a screen placed directly over the print material will remain the same size, regardless of the image magnification.

One benefit of the "sandwich"-type texture screens is the relatively low cost of individual units. Therefore, you can easily afford a collection of textures. It is very simple, also, to sepia- or blue-tone these small screens in a solution of Berg Color Tone or equivalent toner. This toning will provide an added effect of color to the textured background of the print image.

Texture screens can add an extra touch to some images, creating interesting effects. In addition, they can sometimes be used to help improve an otherwise "questionable" transparency. For example, if a slide is slightly unsharp, in some cases the use of a texture screen can create the illusion of better image sharpness. Also, by "sandwiching" a texture screen with a slide you can often add the extra density to a slightly overexposed slide that is necessary to make a satisfactory print. Some examples of the use of texture screens are found in Figure 71 on pages 103–104.

The purist may shun the use of texture screens as a gimmick, but with portraits, some landscapes, and other pictorial subjects, a well-chosen texture screen can definitely add an artistic touch.

Overprinting on Cibachrome

The possibility of overprinting on Cibachrome offers another challenge that, once mastered, will let you enjoy making Christmas or greeting cards, posters or title prints; it will even enable you to include your signature on every print.

The procedure is simple, particularly when printing black letters in a light area of your print (see Figure 72 on page 103). All you need is an overlay sheet of "frosted" acetate on which you have placed your letters and/or numerals from transfer type available at most artists supply stores. Or, you can use a wax lithograph pencil or black ink for your lettering or signing your name. Apply the type or signature to the matte or "frosted" side of the acetate sheet.

If you are using the homemade easel, it can be very simple to register your acetate overlay with the print material. Prior to placing the lettering on the acetate, cut the acetate sheet to the size print you will be making, that is, 8×10 inches, 11×14 inches, etc. Either on a print you have previously made or by projecting the image onto a sheet of white paper or the back of a previous Cibachrome print, indicate where the lettering or signature should be placed.

Once you have finished the lettering and are ready to make the exposure, place a sheet of unexposed Cibachrome-A onto the easel, fit the overlay into position, and make the exposure. There will be no increase in exposure time and no change in filtration.

If the image on which you wish to overprint has a considerable amount of dark area in it and black printing would not be clearly visible, you can reverse the lettering to white or to color, as in the red signature in Figure 72 on page 103. The procedure for reversal of lettering involves two additional steps, but it is not a difficult technique:

1. From your frosted acetate overlay, make a high contrast negative by contact printing. Cut to size, if necessary, to fit the easel, making sure your lettering is in register with the image.

2. Once the negative has been made and opaqued if necessary, make your print as usual. Then remove the slide from the carrier, place the negative overlay on top of the print material, and expose for the second time with the same filtration. The second exposure will completely burn-out the areas under the clear letters of the negative overlay, providing white lettering in the final print image.

In making negative overlays for large-size prints, you do not necessarily have to purchase large-size lith-type films to match the size of the print, but only large enough for the area to be covered by the lettering or titling. Make the negative, then cut out the image and tape it to an opaque cover sheet as shown in Figure 73.

The cover sheet should be cut to the same size as the print you plan to make and the cutouts positioned properly with respect to the desired placement of the lettering. Tape the sections to the back of the cover sheet, then follow the procedure outlined above.

If you prefer colored letters to white, simply tape two or three layers of colored cellophane or acetate over the lettering and expose as discussed above. You will probably need more than one layer of colored material to obtain sufficient density in the print image with a reasonably long exposure.

If you would like to use both positive (black) and negative (white or colored) lettering on the same print, the procedure would be as follows: First expose the print with the frosted acetate overlay; in total darkness remove the slide from the carrier, put the negative film sheet into place, and expose as outlined above.

Figure 73. Illustration showing how a litho negative can be inset into a larger mask for reversal or "drop-out" images on a Cibachrome print. After the main print exposure has been made, the slide should be removed from the carrier, and the litho overlay placed on the Cibachrome material in the dark. Then an exposure is made equal to the main print exposure.

Of course, lettering is not the only thing you can imprint on Cibachrome material; your own imagination will suggest other creative effects obtainable with the overlay technique.

In-Camera Exposure of Cibachrome

Another interesting use of Cibachrome print material that can be utilized with this direct positive material is exposure *in the camera,* but it requires a camera that will accept sheet material. Such cameras could range from a pinhole version, to a 4×5-inch view camera, to a specially constructed unit such as made by Dr. Warren E. Gilson of Middleton, Wisconsin.

Dr. Gilson has been extremely successful in producing 16×20-inch Cibachrome photographs through direct exposure, and museums and art collectors are requesting his services to obtain "permanent" photographs of their works of fine art.

Within ten days of his first use of a 4×5-inch Cibachrome Discovery Kit, in July 1978, Dr. Gilson was making 16×20-inch Cibachrome images directly with a crude "box" camera as illustrated in Figure 74.

His procedure was as follows: "A hole was cut in the end of a 21×21×24-inch cardboard packing carton. A 240mm lens was held in place in the lens hole with twisted wire and rubber bands. The light sources and subject were placed in the box, and by adjusting the various parts, the enlarged image was projected onto a 16×20-inch piece of Cibachrome-A material fastened to the wall. The arrangement was similar to that of an enlarger, with the illuminated subject taking the place of a transparency. The box was

128

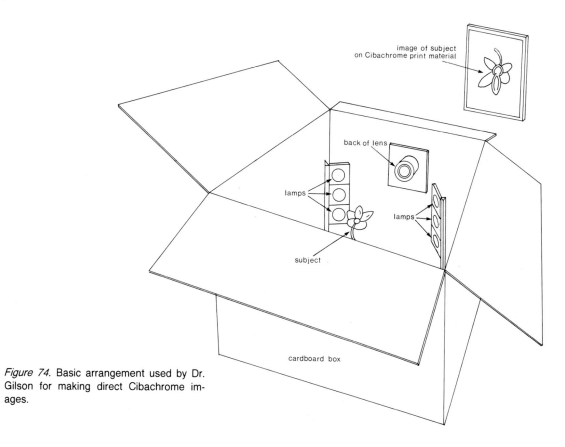

image of subject
on Cibachrome print material

back of lens

lamps

lamps

subject

cardboard box

Figure 74. Basic arrangement used by Dr. Gilson for making direct Cibachrome images.

closed to prevent light leaks. Complete darkness in the room was necessary, as with regular Cibachrome printing." These experiments were described in the July 1979 issue of *Modern Photography.*

One of Dr. Gilson's remarkable photographs is reproduced in Figure 75 on page 104, and you can readily see the sharpness and detail he has achieved with his homemade camera. In using this type of camera setup, the image will be reversed unless a mirror or prism is placed in front of the lens.

Inspired by the success achieved with the homemade camera constructed from a cardboard packing box, Dr. Gilson has designed and constructed a 16×20-inch monorail view camera to expand his capabilities. Similar prototype 11×14-inch cameras, with backs for 8×10-inch holders, have been made with commercial production in mind.

Dr. Gilson offers the following guidelines for in-camera use of Cibachrome-A with indoor lighting: "Illumination, filters, diaphragm setting, and the length of exposure are best determinated by the trial and success method. As a starting point, the following recommendations are suggested: filtration: Y60 M00 C00, four 500-watt photo-ECT 3200K lamps, and with a 240mm focal-length lens, a setting of f/45 at one-minute exposure. The light may be pulsed, that is, on 10 seconds and off 10 seconds. This will prevent burning the filters if they are placed over the lamps and will protect the subject of the photograph. The film responds approximately the same to the interrupted light as to continuous light. Yellow filtration may be added or subtracted, or an addition of cyan or magenta filters may be indicated according to the subject."

Because Cibachrome-A print material has an effective ASA speed of only about 2, in-camera use, such as practiced by Dr. Gilson, is most readily applicable to photographing inanimate objects; otherwise, movement of the subject may cause image blur due to the long exposures required.

It is possible to make instantaneous exposures of life subjects by using electronic flash illumination and large aperture lenses or to immobilize persons by use of old-fashioned props used in the early days of portrait photography. The benefits gained over prints made from well-exposed, sharp 35mm color slides, however, would not be sufficient as a rule to justify the extraordinary measures required for direct portraiture with Cibachrome print material.

At the other extreme from the work of Dr. Gilson is the creative imagery produced by artist Willie Anne Wright of Richmond, Virginia, with Cibachrome-A in a pinhole camera. Wright's work has been exhibited in a number of photographic and art galleries, such as the Virginia Museum of Fine Arts, Southeastern Center of Contemporary Art, and Déjà Vu Gallery of Photographic Art in Toronto, and she is gaining considerable recognition for these pinhole images.

Wright does a considerable amount of her work outdoors, particularly at the beach where there is brilliant light, but additional filters are required to compensate for the difference in daylight color (approximately 5500K) as opposed to the color temperature of photofloods (3400K). With her self-designed 8×10-inch and 16×20-inch pinhole cameras, she generally uses a Hoya K2 (yellow) filter over the pinhole and obtains a "slightly greenish, but acceptable approximation of natural color" as shown in Figure 76 on page 104. With the addition of an 85B filter to the K2, the effect is a "warm, rosy color which is suitable for some subject matter."

Pinhole exposures, even in bright sunlight, are long; Wright's may run from one to five minutes or longer. She writes that it is impossible to predetermine the exact color filtration or exposure in her work because of the difference in filtration from batch to batch of Cibachrome-A print material and the difference in the quality and brilliance of the sunlight from scene to scene. "It is the unpredictable aspects of Cibachrome in a pinhole camera that makes it mysterious and exciting. Each print is unique. The possibilities for creative experimentation are endless."

In between the special 16×20-inch view camera built by Dr. Gilson and the pinhole cameras of Ms. Wright, there is of course the standard 4×5-inch view camera, which a number of photographers use regularly. Cibachrome-A 4×5-inch print material fits easily into standard 4×5-inch film holders and offers a good opportunity for experimentation with in-camera techniques.

Painting with Light

Another exciting creative possibility with the positive-to-positive feature of Cibachrome-A print material is "painting with light." One of the masters of this technique is Mr. George Stadnik of Worcester, Massachusetts. Mr. Stadnik's lumiagraphs, as he calls them, are works of art in light and color and have been exhibited widely in museums and galleries and in permanent installations in mural-size images (see Figure 77 on page 105). Lumiagraphs are light paintings, not photographs. There are no cameras involved in creating the brilliant images. The colors are formed by filtration, refraction, interference, and the additive/subtractive mix of several light beams (including lasers and fiber optics), and form and texture are produced by masking, refraction, or reflection directly onto the Cibachrome material.

The equipment necessary for Mr. Stadnik's lumiagraphs or for your own painting with light is a darkroom, light sources, a variety of lenses for projections, masks, and color filters. Anything that will modify light in some way can, with imagination and work, be used to produce an image. Exposures are flexible, especially in terms of color. Cool colors reach saturation faster than warm colors; therefore, some dodging and sequencing of exposure may be necessary.

Light sources can be as simple as a flashlight with colored filters or cellophane over the lens (for a fine line, simply tape a piece of cardboard or black plastic with a pinhole opening over the flashlight lens) or as complicated as the laser beams and fiber optics used by Mr. Stadnik. Mylar and reflective foils can be simple tools for bouncing colored light onto the print material.

The work of Dr. Gilson, Ms. Wright, and Mr. Stadnik can be an inspiration to all, opening a whole new world of creative use of Cibachrome print material. There are a great number of other photographic artists who have developed their own techniques in using Cibachrome in a variety of different ways to achieve truly beautiful and unusual images.

Your own imagination is the only limit in working with the positive-to-positive system of Cibachrome. In most instances, you can previsualize the effects achievable with this remarkable material, which is one reason it has become the choice of creative photographic workers. Add to that the brilliant colors and the stability of the dye images, and it becomes the ideal medium for a lasting image of your expressive viewpoint.

After the Print

CHAPTER 11

The Finishing Touches

There is no doubt that you will cherish many of your Cibachrome prints and will want to mount them for interior decoration, give them as gifts to your friends, or perhaps even sell them. Adding a few finishing touches can often enhance the final print. In this section, various techniques of retouching, adding surface finishes or textures, mounting the print, and finally matting, framing, and displaying your final efforts will be discussed.

But it is best to start with one of the most prevalent and simplest problems—that of removing fingerprints. There are basically two surfaces with which you will be working with Cibachrome: the Hi-Gloss surface of Cibachrome-A on the triacetate base and the Pearl finish of Cibachrome-A on the RC base. If not handled properly, fingerprints will be more evident on the Hi-Gloss surface than they will be on the RC Pearl finish.

Surface fingerprints generally may be removed with any good film cleaner (do not use movie-film cleaner as it may contain a lubricant); if more drastic means must be employed, rubber cement solvent or lacquer thinner, used sparingly, is excellent. Apply with a soft lintless cloth, such as the white gloves used in the darkroom, or a dampened lens tissue. Do not use Kleenex or other facial tissues, as they have a tendency to scratch the surface on the glossy-type prints. But sometimes there are rather stubborn fingerprints, which are difficult to remove or even imprinted into the emulsion, that may require other means of treatment. In this case, if the print is *unmounted,* re-soak it in clean water (at approximately 75°F), and after two or three minutes, when the emulsion has absorbed water and swelled, gently rub the area with your fingers and smooth out the surface. In most cases, the print will dry, leaving no trace of the fingerprint.

Retouching Cibachrome Prints

There are two types of retouching for photographic prints: "subtractive" and "additive." In subtractive retouching, you will be eliminating color to change it to another color; in "additive" retouching, you may simply add additional color for a more pleasing photograph.

Subtractive Retouching

As the Cibachrome process is a positive-to-positive system, any dust or scratches on your transparency will be reproduced as black spots or lines in the final print. Retouching these black marks can be difficult; the best answer to eliminating them is to avoid them in the first place by being scrupulously clean in making your prints. Check your slide carefully for dust or other matter; if it is scratched, try your skill with one of the liquid scratch removers available at most photo stores.

Admittedly, keeping your prints 100 percent free from black spots is a lot easier said than done, and inevitably there will be occasions when retouching is desirable. The simplest way to eliminate these spots is to cover them with an opaque color that matches the color of the surrounding area. Such an opaque covering may be a thin layer of artists' acrylic or oil paints or Pelikan opaque color. These are available at many art stores. The one disadvantage of this technique is that the colors are not absorbed by the print emulsion; therefore, the retouching becomes quite visible when the print is viewed from an angle. Spraying the print with a clear lacquer after retouching will help correct this problem.

Another technique for removing black spots is to completely bleach them chemically and apply transparent dye of the appropriate color. Cibachrome transparent retouching colors are available in a kit that contains dry, solid tablets in all necessary colors. These dyes are brilliant and light-fast and keep well on storage.

Complete bleaching of a spot in a Cibachrome print may be accomplished as follows, as taken from a technical bulletin from Ilford Inc.

CHEMICALS REQUIRED: sulphuric acid 2N, potassium permanganate, and potassium metabisulphite.

FORMULA: Solution A: sulphuric acid 2N
Solution B: potassium permanganate—16 grams/liter
Solution C: potassium metabisulphite—2% solution

STABILITY: For one day when mixed. In keeping the individual components in storage, the potassium permanganate *must* be stored in a *glass container* only.

PROCEDURE: Mix equal parts of Solution A and Solution B and apply to the spot to be removed for a time period not to exceed 1 1/2 minutes. Blot off any excess solution.

The spots should be bleached away in several applications, rather than all at one time. If after the first application there is still evidence of the spot, add additional bleach as necessary, always blotting any excess solution.

When the spot has been satisfactorily removed, neutralize with Solution C (potassium metabisulphite 2%). Solution C should be applied with a moistened cotton swab to cover the area where the bleach has been applied. Prolonged application of Solution C will destroy the surface of the print!

As soon as the area has been neutralized, wash the entire print in running water for 5 minutes and dry as usual.

COMMENTS: Use rubber resist or photo maskoid around the area to be bleached to protect the surface of the print not to be treated.

NOTE: To make sulphuric acid 2N from concentrated acid, add 20 ml of concentrate to 340 ml of water. NEVER ADD WATER TO THE ACID!

In this bleaching procedure, you are dealing with very strong chemicals and the following CAUTIONS must be carefully read and followed!

Solution A: SULPHURIC ACID 2N

POISON! CORROSIVE! Causes severe burns. Harmful if swallowed or inhaled. Do not get into eyes, on skin, or on clothing. Avoid breathing vapors. Wash hands thoroughly after handling. In case of contact with skin or clothing, wash with soap and water and treat the affected area with sodium bicarbonate (baking soda). When mixing from concentrate, wear rubber gloves and chemical goggles.

KEEP OUT OF REACH OF CHILDREN!

Solution B: POTASSIUM PERMANGANATE

CAUTION! May be harmful if swallowed. Wash thoroughly after handling. In case of contact with skin, rinse thoroughly with soap and water. In case of contact with eyes, flush thoroughly with clean water for at least 15 minutes.

KEEP OUT OF REACH OF CHILDREN!

Solution C: POTASSIUM METABISULPHITE

CAUTION! May cause skin or eye irritation. May be harmful if swallowed.

KEEP OUT OF REACH OF CHILDREN!

Because of the strong chemical activity of the individual components and the mixed bleaching solution, subtractive bleaching should be attempted only by those who will take great care in handling and storing them!

Once the area has been bleached, the retouching dye should be applied with care since it will diffuse into the emulsion and be difficult to remove thereafter. Small areas, such as spots, can be retouched without pre-wetting the print surface, but larger areas should be pre-wetted with water containing a wetting agent such as Photo-Flo 200. Also, in bleaching or retouching larger areas, the surrounding portions of the print should be protected by a stripping lacquer, such as rubber resist or photo maskoid.

In restoring the color of a small spot, make several applications of a dilute dye solution, rather than trying to match the color with one application. When retouching larger areas, the same technique of using dilute colors should be employed, but another problem will be encountered because a wet Cibachrome image takes on a reddish cast, particularly in the shadow areas. This can make the matching of colors somewhat tricky.

After Cibachrome prints have been retouched with Cibachrome transparent dyes, they should be soaked in water for 30 to 40 seconds, and after gentle rubbing with your fingers of the retouched area to remove any excess dye, the print should be hung to dry.

Adding Surfaces or Textures

There are several methods for adding a protective surface coating to a finished Cibachrome print. Surface finishes offer a number of advantages: they protect the print from fingerprints and scratches, may be cleaned with a moist cloth or sponge, extend the life of the image to some extent by absorbing UV radiation and keeping out moisture, and provide a choice of final surface texture.

For example, three different surface finishes can be obtained by applying photographic lacquers found in many photo shops: a high-gloss finish equal to that of an unlacquered print, a luster finish, and a matte finish, which is particularly suitable for portraits.

These lacquers, such as McDonald, are high quality products that will not yellow with age, may be wiped clean with a damp cloth, and give excellent protection from air pollutants, moisture, dust, etc.

Applying a lacquer spray from an aerosol package takes some skill and patience. The smaller the print, generally the easier the job, but when you try a 16×20-inch print, some skill is required.

The general procedure in spraying a print is as follows:

1. Lay the print face-up on a large piece of paper or cardboard as level as possible. (Note: all spraying should be done in well-ventilated areas, which are relatively dust-free, if possible.)

2. Hold the aerosol can at approximately six to eight inches and at an approximate 45-degree angle to the print, then spray slowly and evenly back and forth across the whole print, going about two inches beyond each side of the print.

3. Turn the print at a 90-degree angle and repeat the process.

4. When you finish spraying both in the vertical and horizontal dimensions, there should be an even and wet coating of lacquer over the entire surface of the print.

5. This is perhaps the most important step in the whole spraying process: Walk away from the print and do not return for four to five minutes, by which time the print should be dry. If you stay to watch the print, there is a great temptation to spray it again; if you do so, you can create an uneven surface by applying fresh spray to a partially dried finish.

"Cold" Lamination of Cibachrome Prints

Lamination of a print with a covering of Mylar or similar material should not really be attempted without professional equipment. In the first place, the covering must be placed on the print perfectly evenly, and it must be done in virtually dust-free conditions. One piece of dirt or dust embedded under the lamination can cause a blemish that will spoil the whole appearance. There are a few commercial facilities that can do an excellent job of lamination, but the process is not generally recommended for home use.

"Hot" Lamination of Cibachrome Prints

Another form of lamination is done with a mounting press, is quite simple, and offers a choice of glossy or matte surfaces and an infinite selection of textures. The process, known as Exhibitex® and manufactured by Seal, Inc., is available in many photographic and art stores and can be used to protect the print, as well as for making photographic place mats, coasters, serving trays, etc.

Exhibitex® is sold in kit form, and each package contains all the necessary materials for the process, as well as a representative selection of textures. You may use other textures of your own choice. For example, by simply placing a piece of lace over the Exhibitex® and applying the heat and pressure of a mounting press, the pattern of the lace is embossed in the thermoplastic covering to give an unusual effect to certain subject matter.

The simple and complete instructions for using Exhibitex® are enclosed in every kit, so it is unnecessary to outline them here, but consider these few notes:

1. Exhibitex® is activated by heat, so you will need a mounting press, preferably one with an accurate thermostat and heat control.

2. Temperatures up to 210°F do not normally change the color of the Cibachrome dyes, but *the print must be properly processed according to directions, and final washing must be complete.* If you plan to use Exhibitex® on specific prints, wash the print thoroughly under running water for at least five minutes. Without proper processing and adequate washing, the heat and pressure of a mounting press can cause stains or deterioration of some dyes.

Mounting the Print

Mounting Cibachrome prints made on the Hi-Gloss triacetate base has presented some problems because of the unique nature of the material. In the first place, there is a gelatin layer on the back of the print to which some adhesives do not easily adhere; secondly, the glossy surface of the print is so smooth that it shows every defect in the mounting material, every piece of dirt or matter caught between the print and the mounting material, and every unevenness in the application of adhesive. In spite of these disadvantages, there is not a color material available today that can compare with a correctly made and mounted

Cibachrome print in terms of sharpness, depth, and color. So mounting becomes an important part of the final presentation of your work.

Cibachrome Pearl RC base print material is easier to mount because it responds much the same way as other RC paper-base products. And the luster surface helps in minimizing the problems encountered with the glossy surface material.

The type of mounting for a print is governed primarily by the plan for its ultimate use or display. For instance, with much interest now in preservation and archival storage of photographic images, many museums and galleries prefer not to mount prints permanently, but to "hinge" them at the top to acid-free "archival" mount boards with an "archival" mat inside a metal frame for exhibition. This type of mounting will keep the print flat and aid in preserving the image under controlled temperature and humidity conditions. Many darkroom workers are not interested in this kind of protection, preferring that their photographs be mounted attractively for home decoration and for competitive or commercial purposes.

Choice of Mounting Supports

A variety of mounting supports are available today, including the following:

1. Mounting board: A cardboard material, this is available in both single weight and double weight at most art stores. This type of mount is probably the most widely used material for print mounting and the least expensive. Also available in many stores will be "archival" mount boards, an acid-free composition especially made for preservation of photographic images.

Disadvantages are that the cardboard surface has a slight "texture" and is not as smooth as it may appear, and there is a tendency to curl, especially when it is used in a mounting press.

2. Masonite: This is a rigid fiberboard, available at most lumber supply houses. For utmost rigidity and resistance to warping under humid conditions, it is recommended that you specify 1/4-inch tempered Masonite, which is particularly suitable for flush mounting photographs. Some suppliers, such as Coda, Inc., offer a Masonite-type product with a self-adhesive material ready for use.

3. Ilford Mounting Panels: These white plastic panels come in the following formats: 4×5-inch double weight, 8×10-inch single and double weight, and 11×14-inch double weight self-adhesive mounts with a very smooth surface, available at Ilford dealers. The special adhesive has been thoroughly tested in controlled heat/cold and high and low humidity conditions with excellent results. Ilford mounting panels are primarily designed for flush mounting, and complete instructions are included with each package.

4. Aluminum: Some suppliers now offer thin but rigid self-adhesive aluminum panels designed for flush mounting. The aluminum base offers the best protection against warping under all weather conditions. One supplier is Z-Mounts, Inc. of Elmsford, N. Y.

5. Foamcore and Gatorboard: These are lightweight mounting materials consisting of two smooth paper surfaces with a plastic foam inner core. Foamcore is available in approximately 1/4-inch thickness from many art stores. It can be used in a dry-mounting press

despite the foam center, but its main disadvantage is that it is easily dented. Gatorboard, on the other hand, is more substantial, has a slightly smoother surface, and is available in more substantial thicknesses.

6. Plexiglas: Plexiglas, particularly when black, can provide the most dramatic of all mounting materials for a Cibachrome print. The surface is smooth, and the high gloss of the material itself closely matches the reflectance quality of a Cibachrome Hi-Gloss print. In fact, an 8 × 10-inch Cibachrome print mounted on a 14 × 16-inch piece of black Plexiglas (or any similar size with wide borders) and properly lighted can give the appearance of a back-lighted transparency when viewed from a distance! The disadvantages of Plexiglas are its high cost, attraction for dust particles, and susceptibility to scratches. But all in all, Plexiglas may well be considered the ultimate for the dramatic presentation of the brilliance of a Cibachrome print.

7. Canvas: Both Cibachrome Hi-Gloss and the Cibachrome RC Pearl finishes may be mounted directly on canvas with the proper mounting press. The Hi-Gloss Cibachrome requires a special mounting press with great pressure, such as the McDonald or Ademco presses, because of the hardness and lack of resilience of the plastic base. Each of these brands requires different techniques and adhesives, and manufacturers' directions should be closely followed.

With the Cibachrome RC base, the print should be "stripped," that is, the back layer of polyethylene removed from the base, and a press with great pressure used in order to obtain maximum texture in the finished work. The Pearl finish and canvas texture are particularly effective with portraits.

Choice of Adhesives

Several types of adhesives are available for mounting Cibachrome prints, the choice depending somewhat on the permanency you may desire. There are also two methods of mounting: "cold" mounting, which does not require heat, and "hot" mounting, which needs a mounting press or some other form of heat.

"Cold" Mounting

Taking everything into consideration, "cold" mounting of Cibachrome prints should be considered the preferred method. It requires less equipment—particularly of the expensive kind—is simpler to accomplish, and there is less chance of damaging the print.

Among the techniques of "cold" mounting are these:

1. Spray mounting adhesives: Several manufacturers market excellent adhesives in spray cans, among them the 3M Company and Seal, Inc. The Scotch® brand Photomount Adhesive by the 3M Company is a clear adhesive available in 8 oz. and 16 oz. cans at most dealers. The Seal Print Spray™ is a new acid-free all-purpose spray mounting adhesive available in 16 oz. cans.

The advantage of spray adhesives is their ease in use, but follow the manufacturers' directions carefully for best results, as "setting" or drying times before the sprayed print is mounted to the board may differ between various brands of adhesive. Generally speaking, for a more permanent mount, even coatings of the spray on both the back of the print and the mount are required.

A troubleshooting guide from a Product Information Bulletin on 3M's mounting adhesives is given below.

TROUBLESHOOTING

PROBLEM	POSSIBLE CAUSE	REMEDY
Prints lift or bubble	Insufficient adhesive	Increase amount applied. About 35–40 sq. ft./can is recommended coverage
	Print and mount board not conditioned before mounting	Condition both in same atmosphere for several hours before mounting
	Mounted print taken into humid atmosphere after mounting	Condition 24 hours in same atmosphere after mounting
	Textured surface of print or mounting surface	Requires heavier adhesive coating to fill voids in surface
	Adhesive applied to photos or other nonporous surfaces not allowed to dry thoroughly before mounting	Wait 5 minutes after spraying before mounting to let solvents escape
	Stresses not removed before mounting (curl, folds, wrinkles)	Remove stresses and flatten print before mounting
	Mounting on hardboard. Oils in board will soften spray adhesives	Use on recommended surfaces
Can't get all of the adhesive out of the can	Dip tube is not lined up properly	Line up spray tip with dot on can rim
Spray "spits" when applied	Can not shaken well before using	Shake can well and test spray before starting
Can will not spray	Spray tip plugged up	Tip can upside down and purge after use. Tip may also require cleaning with solvent

Another advantage of the spray method is the relative ease in removing the print from the mount at a later time, if so desired, by carefully lifting one corner of the print and applying rubber cement solvent or thinner along the adhered surface until it softens and loosens from the support. A plastic bottle with a long needle dispenser is ideal for this procedure.

Disadvantages may include the lack of real permanency over a long period of years in holding the print securely on the mount, especially in areas where heat and humidity can be a problem. Even when both print and mount are sprayed—in which case a mat must be used to cover the excess adhesive on the mount-board support—the print can buckle under heat and humidity conditions unless the print is framed or otherwise protected. The Cibachrome RC print material will retain its flatness and bond better than the Cibachrome Hi-Gloss triacetate material.

2. Positionable Mounting Adhesive #567: Another product offered by the 3M Company is #567, a unique adhesive formulation that is easy to use and enables you to position or reposition your print a number of times before making a permanent bond. Simple and complete directions are listed on every package, and you will find #567 (or #568 in roll form) at many photographic and art supply dealers. According to 3M's specifications, it is recommended for photographs up to 16×20 inches in size and will not dry out, stain, or discolor prints. It is an acid-free formulation, made from synthetic, acrylic polymer.

A troubleshooting guide for use of Positionable Mounting Adhesive #567 from 3M's Product Information Bulletin is given below.

TROUBLESHOOTING
Pressure Applied By Hand

PROBLEM	POSSIBLE CAUSE	REMEDY
Poor adhesive transfer from carrier sheet	Insufficient burnishing pressure	Increase burnishing pressure
	Using hand roller or soft squeegee	Use 3M T-639 plastic squeegee
	Finger oils or other contaminant on surface	Clean off with solvent
Bond failure	Insufficient burnishing pressure	Increase burnishing pressure
	Use of hand roller or soft squeegee	Use 3M T-639 plastic squeegee
	Item exceeds size limitations for No. 567 (16"×20")	Use Promount or Vac-U-Mount
	Used on non-recommended materials	Consult instructions and change adhesives
	Curl, wrinkles or folds in item	Stress—relieve before mounting

Seal, Inc. has introduced an acid-free cold-mounting pressure-sensitive adhesive by the name of Print Mount™, available in both sheet and roll form. It, too, is repositionable, and it is claimed that the bond grows stronger with age.

With both 3M's #567 and Seal's Print Mount™, the ultimate bond between the photograph and the mount occurs approximately 24 hours after the actual mounting has been done, and it would be advisable to keep the mounted print under weight to assure maximum adhesion.

3. Adhesive sheets: This class of adhesives is descriptive of double-sided pressure-

sensitive material covered by two sheets of release paper. There are several brands of adhesive sheets on the market, and the manufacturers' recommendations should be followed. The general procedure is to remove one side of release paper and attach the exposed adhesive side to the back of the print with a print roller, making sure to get an even bond without air bubbles. When this is accomplished, remove the remaining release sheet and attach the print to the mount, again with a print roller, working carefully to smooth the print into place without creating air bubbles.

The one difficulty with this type of adhesive is that once the adhesive touches a surface, it sticks! It is a tough job to remove the print without disturbing the smoothness of the adhesive layer or cracking the print, and extreme care should be used in mounting with this material.

"Hot" Mounting

"Hot" mounting refers to the use of heat in mounting a print, preferably with a mounting press, such as Seal, Ademco, Technal, or McDonald, and special adhesives sold by the manufacturers of these presses.

With some print material, hot mounting may be accomplished with small-size photographs by using a regular iron, but extreme care should be used in applying the iron with even pressure and heat over the entire print. In general, it is not recommended for exhibition prints, particularly with Cibachrome Hi-Gloss material. For best results with Cibachrome-A, even pressure and even heat should be applied to the entire print in a single operation. Moreover, the print should be dried out first by a brief pre-treatment in the press. Acid-free cover sheets should be used.

Mounting Presses

As noted above, there are a numbers of brands of presses available through photo dealers, and all brands come in a variety of sizes and models. Any good mounting press should be satisfactory for mounting your prints, so if you plan to purchase a mounting press, carefully check the specifications of each model to best fit your own personal needs.

Mounting Tissues

Mounting tissues are the thin adhesive sheets used with the press in the final mounting operation, and there are a number of brands and types. Among the brands available that will work well with Cibachrome prints are Colormount®, Fusion®, and Exhibitex® by Seal, the Scotch® Promount heat-activated adhesive by 3M, and Technal. Your photo dealer will have a selection from which to choose. In using any particular mounting tissue, follow the manufacturer's recommendations for best results.

To give you some idea of the specific qualities of various mounting tissues, following is a tabulation on three different brands offered by Seal, Inc., with recommendations for mounting:

BRAND	RECOMMENDED TEMPERATURE	RECOMMENDED TIME BY SIZE	CIBACHROME HI-GLOSS	CIBACHROME RC-PEARL
Colormount	200°–210°F	8×10, 11×14 1–1 1/2 minutes	recommended	recommended
		11×14, 16×20 1 1/2–2 minutes	recommended	recommended
Fusion	180°–210°F	8×10, 11×14 at 180°–200° F 1 1/2–2 minutes	recommended	recommended
		8×10, 11×14 at 200°–210° F 1–1 1/2 minutes	recommended	recommended
		11×14, 16×20 at 180°–200° F 2–2 1/2 minutes	recommended	recommended
		11×14, 16×20 at 200°–210° F 1 1/2–2 minutes	recommended	recommended
Exhibitex Thermoplastic Film	200°–210°F	8×10/1 minute 11×14/1 1/2 min. 16×20/2 min.	recommended	NOT recommended

Each of these three tissues has different characteristics and a different type of bond. Colormount, for example, has a paper base that will shear in the center when peeled off. Fusion has a film base that in itself will not shear, but that can be pulled away from the triacetate base of Cibachrome-A (Hi-Gloss) when peeled. The thermoplastic base of Exhibitex has been designed to stick to the gelatin layer on the back of the triacetate base, and gives the best bond by far for Cibachrome-A Hi-Gloss, but is not recommended for Cibachrome-A Pearl RC base.

Colormount and Fusion tissues are not recommended for mounting prints exceeding 16×20 inches in size, as the shrinkage of the print on cooling can shear the bondline. Exhibitex Thermoplastic Film, however, can be used to mount prints of any size.

Some tips and cautions on hot mounting Cibachrome prints:

1. Make sure the platen of your press is perfectly smooth and clean to avoid any tiny dents or impressions in the surface of the print.

2. Always preheat both the print and the mounting board to remove any excess moisture.

3. Always use a cover sheet over the face of the print so that the heated platen of the press does not come into direct contact with the emulsion surface. With glossy prints, it is recommended that a glossy release film, such as Colormount Cover Sheet or Exhibitex Glossy Film, be used over the emulsion surface, as a matte finish release paper or cover

sheet can have a dulling effect, particularly if the emulsions are soft (when subjected to heat).

4. After mounting, place the mounting board under heavy weight to avoid excess curling of the board during the cooling process.

5. Be sure that any print placed under heat has been properly processed and washed thoroughly under running water, as any residue chemicals can cause staining or color shifts.

6. Choose the mounting board carefully and try to get as smooth a surface as possible. With Cibachrome-A Hi-Gloss, in particular, all the irregularities and the surface texture of the board will be evident in the mounted print. Cibachrome-A Pearl tends to hide some of these problems because of its luster surface and the greater resiliency of its base. Even though the ''hot'' mounting process can give you a good bond for your prints, the one big objection is the curl in the mounting board after the print has cooled. This is not as evident with Cibachrome-A RC Pearl as with the Hi-Gloss, which has far different cooling and shrinkage coefficients than the mount itself; therefore, curling is almost inevitable.

Edging, a Final Touch

There are some Cibachrome workers who like to add a final touch to their prints, especially if the print is flush-mounted and not to be matted. For those who make borderless prints or even prints with black borders, a very thin white line can be added around the border simply by taking a single-edge razor blade and ''scraping'' a narrow line of the emulsion along the four sides of the print.

This is quite simple with a flush-mounted print on any type of rigid mount, such as Ilford mounting panels, Masonite, or even mat board. As shown in the illustrations, hold a single-edge razor blade at a 45-degree angle and pull the blade toward you, carefully removing a narrow line of the emulsion.

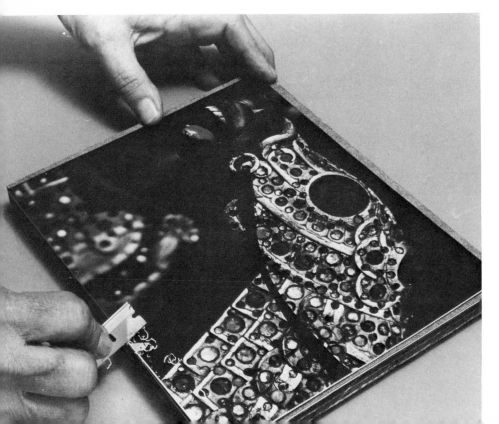

Figure 78. Edging a Cibachrome print can be an attractive final touch, as it provides a thin white line as a border to enhance the appearance. With Hi-Gloss Cibachrome-A, the emulsion is removed easily and smoothly by holding a single-edge razor blade at a 45-degree angle and simply scraping a thin line from the print. The print should be mounted or held on a rigid base during this procedure.

With Cibachrome-A RC base, however, the edge may be a little ragged, and it must be finished off by sanding with a block covered with fine sandpaper until the edges are smooth.

With the Cibachrome-A Hi-Gloss on the triacetate plastic base, the emulsion is removed easily and smoothly in a straight line to give a nice added touch to the print. With the Cibachrome-A RC Pearl, however, the line may be somewhat ragged, and you must finish it off by using a small block covered with a fine sandpaper to smooth off the edges.

Presentation of Cibachrome Prints

The final presentation of your Cibachrome prints will depend largely upon your personal objective. For competition or gallery exhibition, prints are generally mounted on cardboard and may or may not be matted. The selection of the color of the mat or mount board should enhance rather than detract from the print itself. To take a tip from professional picture framers, choose a color that picks up one of the more subtle colors in the print.

On the other hand, if you are most interested in dramatizing the brilliance of color in a Cibachrome print, a dark brown or even black mat or mount board will tend to focus the viewers' eyes directly on the print and its vivid colors.

One effective way of obtaining a somewhat three-dimensional feeling to your mounted prints is to first flush-mount the print, edge it, and then attach the print to a mat board. The thicker the base of your flush mount, the more effective the final presentation. The double-weight Ilford mounting panel is ideal for this purpose.

Unusual and even spectacular print displays can be produced from certain types of slides by assembling two or four prints of the same slide in a "mirror" print or "print quadrant" assembly, as shown in Figures 80 and 81 on page 106.

For home decoration, there are two schools of thought: one says that prints should be attractively matted and framed for best effect and protection of the print; the other insists that a photographic image should stand on its own merit and is best displayed flush-mounted. The solution is really a matter of personal preference; you will have to decide which route you wish to take.

In framing photographic prints, use a mat between the glass and the print; otherwise, the print emulsion may stick to the glass in time.

Another consideration in framing Cibachrome prints is the choice of glass. We are well aware of the problem of reflections from regular glass; to overcome it many people prefer the so-called "non-glare" kind. Unfortunately, the tendency of non-glare glass is to have a dulling effect on an image and it subdues some of the brilliance of a Cibachrome print.

Now available through selected dealers (such as Edmund Scientific, Barrington, N.J.) is a superior type of glass called Denglas, which eliminates the reflections of regular glass, yet does not affect the color quality of the photographic image. Furthermore, it provides some additional protection from UV radiation.

If you prefer the flush-mounted prints in favor of framed prints, here are a few tips:

1. Prior to mounting the print, either spray it with lacquer or laminate it with a material such as Exhibitex. The emulsion surface must be protected against fingerprints, moisture, and fumes.

2. Mount the print on a smooth surface, such as an Ilford mounting panel.

3. Edge the print.

4. With a good glue or epoxy, attach the mounted print to a piece of 1/2- or 3/4-inch plywood or flake-board, cut to the exact size of the print.

5. To cover the exposed sides of the plywood or flake-board, use flexible glue-on Wood Trim by Weldwood or a similar type of edging. Wood Trim is real wood veneer and is available in a variety of types, such as birch, walnut, oak, mahogany, and fir. For further enhancement, you may want to stain the veneer before gluing it to the sides of the block. Colored plastic tape can be substituted for the wood veneer.

The resultant flush-mounted print is simple in presentation, but a very elegant way to display your prized prints.

Storage, display and preservation of Cibachrome prints

One of the most important properties of Cibachrome prints, one that is of special concern and value to photographers and collectors, is the excellent stability of the azo dye images and their freedom from staining. All available evidence indicates that Cibachrome prints will not change under normal dark-storage conditions and will not fade perceptibly for appreciable periods of time when displayed indoors under recommended conditions of illumination. It must be remembered, however, that the dark and light stability of Cibachrome prints is influenced by several factors. These will be examined and the recommended storage and display conditions will be defined.

The Cibachrome azo dyes have considerably better dark and light stability than the azomethine dyes used in chromogenic color materials. In fact, Cibachrome prints have considerably better image stability than all other normally used color films and color paper materials. This superior stability is ascribable to several structural properties of the azo dye molecules, but especially to their higher symmetry and their freedom from polarization, as shown below.

Azo dye   Azomethine dye

Bond energy in Kcal/mol

Figure 79.

Aggregation of the azo dye molecules in Cibachrome image layers provides a further increase in light stability as well as resistance to diffusion. The azo groups are more resistant to oxidation than to reduction, but it requires special conditions to effect reduction. For example, a combination of strong illumination and high moisture can bring about the splitting of the azo group as a result of a photo-reduction reaction. This reaction can be catalyzed by heavy metals, such as iron, and is influenced by the state of dye aggregation as well as by the properties of the binder material (gelatin) and the support. Under normal conditions of temperature and relative humidity, however, the azo dye images are very stable. In fact, Cibachrome prints stored in the dark at a relative humidity below 50 percent and at temperatures below 68°F (20°C) are expected to have archival permanence, provided only that the recommended processing procedures were used. This estimate is based on numerous accelerated aging tests as well as on the performance of actual prints kept under normal room conditions for the past 35 years.

The question is often asked, exactly how long will a Cibachrome print last? No simple, precise answer can be given because the keeping quality of any color photographic image will be influenced by many factors that cannot be accurately assessed beforehand. However, it is possible to define the factors which will have the greatest impact on keeping quality and which should be controlled if the longest possible life is desired.

Factors which influence the keeping quality of Cibachrome images

The factors that have the greatest influence on the dark and light stability of Cibachrome image dyes are tabulated below.

DARK STORAGE
- Relative humidity
- Temperature
- Atmospheric pollutants—for example, sulfur dioxide or ammonia gas
- Microorganisms—for example, fungi or spores

DISPLAY
- Irradiation—intensity, spectral distribution and duration of the radiation, i.e., light and ultraviolet
- Relative humidity
- Temperature
- Atmospheric pollutants (as above)
- Microorganisms (as above)

Usually, a combination of several of these factors or of all of them must be considered. In the dark, a combination of very high temperature (above 80°C) and high humidity (above 60 percent relative humidity) is required to cause a degradation of the azo dye aggregates in Cibachrome prints. (Under such extreme conditions, the triacetate and polyester supports of Cibachrome prints are degraded also.) High temperature by itself will not produce any change in the dye image. For example, no measurable change in dye density occurs when Cibachrome prints are kept at 194°F (90°C) for four weeks as long as the relative humidity is maintained below 50 percent.

The concentration of industrial gases (sulfur dioxide, etc.) would have to be quite high over prolonged periods of time to cause serious degradation of Cibachrome prints, because the azo dyes are quite resistant to their actions. As for the microorganisms, fungus or bacterial growth can and will occur when prints are kept under high humidity conditions, especially at elevated temperatures. The gelatin of the image layers is a fertile medium for microorganisms under such tropical atmospheric conditions. For this reason and others cited above, high relative humidity should be avoided.

Very low relative humidity is also undesirable because gelatin becomes brittle when it dries out. Therefore, *the recommended dark-storage conditions for Cibachrome prints are:* a temperature below 68°F (20°C) and a relative humidity of from 30 to 50 percent. Industrial gases and microorganisms should be excluded through proper air filtration. If these conditions are maintained, and if the prints have been processed properly and have not been mounted on or with offensive materials, they can be expected to have archival permanence.

Light stability

The light stability of Cibachrome images has been investigated extensively under natural and simulated daylight as well as under fluorescent and tungsten light. The spectral distribution and intensity of these three common types of illumination vary considerably and so, therefore, does the required time of exposure before a perceptible change in color is observed in Cibachrome prints displayed under one or the other illumination, or their mixtures. Moreover, the ultraviolet content of these illuminants varies appreciably, sunlight having the highest and tungsten light the lowest amount of ultraviolet radiation. Also, the relative humidity of the air comes into play because the destructive photo-reduction reaction will be initiated under high humidity strong light conditions.

The total energy of the light falling on a print can be measured by a suitable radiation monitor. The quantity of light in such measurements is expressed in calories per cm² or Langley. Test measurements of this kind made under different conditions of illumination have shown that the dye density of an unprotected Cibachrome print will decrease by 10 percent after it has received about 10,000 Langley of light and by about 15 percent with 15,000 Langley. A 15 percent loss in dye density is usually acceptable, especially since the three dyes fade at about the same rate. This means that the image changes primarily in overall density rather than in color balance. With very critical subjects and delicate tints, however, a 10 percent density change may be the maximum permissible loss.

The table below provides data on the approximate periods of time required to accummulate 10,000 Langley of light outdoors in the temperate zone, indoors at various distances from a window and indoors without daylight.

APPROXIMATE PERIODS OF ILLUMINATION TO REACH 10,000 LANGLEY

OUTDOORS		SUMMER	WINTER	AVERAGE
at 45° angle toward south		20 days	60 days	1 month
INDOORS	**DISTANCE FROM WINDOW**			
direct sun half day	20 cm (8 in.)	200 days	600 days	1 year
no direct sun	20 cm (8 in.)	400 days	1,200 days	2 years
no direct sun	2 m (6 ft.)			5 years
	4 m (12 ft.)			10 years
continuous fluorescent light—300 lux (no daylight)				12 years
continuous tungsten light—250 lux (no daylight)				15 years

It will be evident from the above data that Cibachrome prints should not normally be displayed outdoors and certainly not in direct sunlight. If prints must be displayed outdoors, however, they should not only be shielded from direct sunlight, but should be protected also against moisture by a suitable lacquer coating, plastic foil cover or through embedment in fiberglass. These materials can also provide added protection against ultraviolet radiation.

Indoors it is important to minimize direct exposure to sunlight through proper placement of prints. Similarly, intense artificial light should not be directed at prints for prolonged periods of time. If these cautions are observed, Cibachrome prints can be expected to show no perceptible change in color quality for about 10 years in a daylight-lit room and for about 15 years if no delicate, critical image densities are involved.

The expected life of unprotected Cibachrome prints under bright fluorescent or tungsten illumination is from 25 to 50 years, assuming that the lamps will be operated for 12 hours a day and that the permissible change in dye density ranges from 10 to 15 percent. It is assumed also that the room temperature and particularly the relative humidity will be at reasonable levels most of the time.

In conclusion, while there are no absolutely permanent organic dyes, the azo dyes used in Cibachrome materials provide excellent long-term dark stability and very good light stability, provided only that proper processing is employed. The dark stability can be enhanced by storage under optimum conditions of relative humidity (30–50 percent) and temperature (below 68°F) and by the exclusion of industrial gases and microorganisms. The light stability can be enhanced by a factor of two to three times by exclusion of moisture and ultraviolet radiation, e.g., through the application of protective lacquers or plastic foils. No significant staining of whites will occur in dark or light storage if processing is carried out in accordance with recommendations.

Index